OFFENSIVE
and
DEFENSIVE
LINE PLAY

OFFENSIVE
and
DEFENSIVE
LINE PLAY

GOMER JONES

Athletic Director
and
Head Football Coach,
University of Oklahoma

Englewood Cliffs, N. J.
PRENTICE-HALL, INC.

*Library of Congress
Catalog Card Number: 61-10059*

First Printing.....February, 1961
Second Printing..September, 1961
Third Printing........June, 1962
Fourth Printing.......April, 1964
Fifth Printing.........May, 1965

PRINTED IN THE UNITED STATES OF AMERICA

63066—BC

Foreword

From the days of George Sanford, under Walter Camp at Yale, and Ernest (Pot) Graves, under first, Percy D. Haughton at Harvard, and later, Charles D. Daly at West Point, on down through the modern era, the countless superior teams, individual stars and technical advancement of that matchless game, intercollegiate football, have traced their success in great measure to the work of a devoted, yet relatively unsung, group of great line coaches. In the very top echelon of these architects of the game stands the name of Gomer T. Jones, of the University of Oklahoma.

The astonishing 14-year story of Oklahoma Football under Charles B. (Bud) Wilkinson is the result of selfless dedication by coaches and players and an implemented understanding that the game, as intended to be played (in the colleges, at least), is primarily one of conditioned, intelligent movement. For it is only through such dedication and such movement that there can ever be the emphatic blocking and tackling that are indispensable to—indeed, are the essence of—victory.

In the ability to impart such dedication by example and such movement by instruction, Gomer Jones (just a plain, shrewd old country boy, who will blush at these words) stands, in my opinion, unsurpassed. In their work of several years ago, *Modern Defensive Football*, Co-Authors Jones and Wilkinson made a contribution that benefitted teachers of the game at all levels. They will now find *Offensive and Defensive Line Play* by Gomer T. Jones an equally rewarding, in fact, an exciting experience.

TIM COHANE

... So Goes the Team

Ever since the game of American football became a part of our sports life, studious observers have realized that the foundation of a successful team rests on the linemen. The "infantrymen" who battle on each play, toe to toe along the line of scrimmage, are the critical factors in the success of a team.

Football, in a sense, is warfare in miniature. The rival armies attack and defend a given piece of ground. It is true that the forward pass and kicking add the Air Force to the game and require defense and attack "in depth"; but as students of military history have long noted, the infantryman must take and occupy the land if the battle is to be won.

This concept is totally applicable to the game of football. When your team is on offense, if your linemen can attack and move forward into the ground of the enemy, you will have a successful offense. Your team will be able to move the ball to the goal line and score. Conversely, if, when on defense, your linemen stop the attack of the enemy by successfully defending their territory, the opponents will be unable to score. Your team will win.

To summarize the statement above—the fundamental basic foundation of a successful football team is the ability of the line. If your line can win the fight over the opponent's line, your team will win the game. If your line loses the fight to the opponent's line, you will lose the game.

In preparing this book, I have divided the subject matter into three basic phases. These are: 1) Basic Line Drills and Selection of Personnel; 2) Offensive Techniques and Drills; 3) Defensive Fundamentals and Drills.

The thoughts and ideas which I have presented in this book are for the most part the product of my experience as a player and a coach. A great deal of the material has been learned from others, and I would like to acknowledge my great debt to those people who have played such a vital role in my growth of understanding concerning this game.

My college football participation was under one of America's truly great coaches—Francis Schmidt at Ohio State University. I had the good fortune, after graduation, to be a member of Coach Schmidt's staff and work with Ernie Godfrey, his outstanding line coach. The basis of line play described in this book was learned at that time.

During World War II, I was an officer in the Navy's V-5 program. Although I had not participated in football for some six years, I did play again for St. Mary's Pre-Flight Air-Devil team. This rare, unusual experience gave me the opportunity of testing in actual practice the theories concerning line play which I had been teaching as a football coach following my graduation from Ohio State. Thus, in a sense, I had an opportunity personally, in the laboratory of competition, to weigh and measure the relative merits of different types of stance, charge, block protection, and other aspects of line play at a time when I had accumulated a reasonable amount of background knowledge concerning football.

In my opinion, this "graduate competition" was perhaps the most valuable single incident in my education as a coach. It is unusual indeed for any man to have the opportunity to play himself following five years of coaching. At this point in a career, one knows the game well enough to test in practice the theories he has developed while teaching.

Following World War II, I coached one year with Ernie Masterson at the University of Nebraska prior to coming to Oklahoma in the spring of 1947. Since that time I have been the line coach for the Sooners under Head Coach Bud Wilkinson.

The fact that I have been asked to write this book is not a tribute so much to my coaching as it is to the morale, ability, and dedication of the linemen who have played for me at Oklahoma. These men, through their efforts, have made Oklahoma a fine football team over the past decade. Their success as players has been a tribute to their ability and attitude toward the game rather than to my ability as coach.

I will be everlastingly grateful for the opportunity of associating with these fine men. It is my fervent hope that the men who will take their places in the years ahead will have the same sense of loyalty and dedication to our team as did their predecessors. Should this be the case, our team will continue to be a championship contender.

GOMER T. JONES
Norman, Oklahoma

Table of Contents

OFFENSIVE
and
DEFENSIVE
LINE PLAY

CHAPTER ONE

What Makes a Lineman

What are the characteristics of a football lineman? This is a difficult question because the factors are so interrelated that it is virtually impossible to isolate them and talk about them one at a time as you would if you could dissect and analyze them. Obviously, the vital qualifications for success as a football lineman are size, speed, intelligence, and motivation.

In my opinion, motivation—the proper mental attitude—is the essential ingredient. If a young man has a sincere desire to learn, if he is willing to take the hard knocks of the game, if he will strive everlastingly to improve, he may someday reach his goal of being a skillful player in every respect.

If he does not care, if he is lackadaisical in his approach to football, he will never have the tenacity to play well—particularly when he is tired. In the game of football, all players become tired. It is impossible to play without a degree of fatigue. This factor is doubly true in practice. A man who does not care, who loafs and coasts, cannot become a fine football lineman, regardless of his potentials.

If a player has the earnestness—a true sense of purpose—the physical factors begin to become important. Most people feel size is the most important factor. Size is an asset. A good big man is always better than the good little man in a physical contest. However, size and speed are usually counter-balancing skills. The larger the man is, the slower he is likely to be. Conversely, the smaller the man is, the quicker and faster he is likely to be.

There have been many great football linemen who were small. Perhaps the most famous of all was Burt Metzger, Notre Dame's famous "Watch Charm" guard who played under Knute Rockne in the late '20's.

Since that time there have been a number of other men with the same physical characteristics. In common, they have all had the great motivation and desires spoken of above. While they were small, they more than made up for this lack of size through their terrific speed.

If a young man is quick enough and fast enough, he can, in football, defeat much larger opponents. However, small men must recognize that if they are to defeat bigger opponents they must develop their speed to the fullest possible extent. Men gifted with large physiques must realize that this alone will not insure their success as linemen. They must work constantly to develop balance, quickness, and speed. If they have these qualities in equal amount with lighter men, their size will enable them to win the contest.

The professional football players of today are great athletes in the true meaning of the phrase. They are men of tremendous physique. Most of them weigh around 240 pounds. Yet in spite of this tremendous bulk they move as agilely and as quickly as the proverbial cat.

It is a rare thing in high school or in college to find a single man on the entire squad with this type of size and speed. Most players are slightly above average in size and still possess good speed. The two factors are interrelated and a player who wishes to develop must constantly make an effort to improve his speed in every action since his size is an innate growth factor over which he has little or no control.

The final factor is that of intelligence. Unless a man has a quick analytical mind, he will find himself unable to adjust to the rapidly changing situations presented a modern football lineman on both offense and defense.

In summary, the physical and mental characteristics required for successful line play are true motivation, size, speed, and intelligence.

Football is a game of movement and a game of fundamentals. If a lineman is to play successfully he must possess certain fundamental physical skills. A game of football is made up of three basic fundamentals. These are movement (running), blocking, and tackling. A football player in any position must be able to execute these fundamentals flawlessly. On the offense he must move and then block. On defense he must move and then attack. The men who are able to execute these maneuvers successfully will become the outstanding players.

Linemen are usually close to the man they will contact. Their physical skills on every play are somewhat the same, regardless of whether they are playing on offense or defense. Each lineman must strive to master the following points: 1) an explosive start, 2) perfect body control, 3) ability to move in any direction, 4) keep the eyes open, 5) be in a solid hitting position at the point of contact, 6) deliver a blow, and, 7) follow through the area of contact.

It is impossible to over-evaluate the importance of the explosive start. If you can contact your opponent before he moves, while he is still in a stationary position, obviously you can control and master him. In order to start explosively, a lineman must have a good stance.

The stance will vary, depending on the charge to be used. But from his stance each lineman must endeavor to explode as the ball moves, in an effort to beat his opponent to the punch.

While making this explosive start, it is necessary for the player to maintain perfect control of his body. If you charge so hard that you are off balance, you will fall to the ground if your opponent steps to the side and avoids you. On the ground, you are unable to move. Consequently, you are unable to play.

There is an interesting paradox here. The harder a man charges, the less balance he is likely to have. The more balance he has— the less power he will have in his charge. In developing his skills, the lineman should try to maintain balance at all times while he gradually increases his ability to explode at the start of the play.

On offense, a lineman usually knows in what direction he will move as the play starts. However, the charge of the defensive man may cause him to adjust his angle of movement.

On defense, since the defensive lineman does not know where

the ball will go, he can not know exactly where he will move in order to tackle. Obviously, he must be able to adjust the angle of his movement.

Thus, whether playing offense or defense, the football lineman must, after making an explosive start, maintain perfect control of his body so that he can move in the desired direction without loss of time or taking steps in the wrong direction.

It is a human instinct to close the eyes whenever an individual is close to contact. This is a reflex built up through eons of evolution to protect the priceless sight of man. In contact sports, if the eyes are closed in the area of contact, it is impossible to play successfully. When the eyes are closed the player is blind. If he is blind, he cannot see his opponent. In a football game, in the area of contact, the opponent is usually making violently evasive maneuvers. If a player closes his eyes and thereby loses sight of his opponent, he will not be able to adjust to the opponent's moves since he will not have his vision. He will be playing "blind". *Obviously, a lineman cannot play effectively unless he learns to keep his eyes open.*

Football is a game of contact. The team that hits the hardest usually wins. When playing on the line, men either hit, or they get hit. If you are to deliver a hard enough blow to knock your opponent back, you must be in body position which will enable you to use all of your muscles in a co-ordinated manner to deliver the most forceful blow of which you are capable. This position is known as the "hitting position." It will be discussed at greater length later. Briefly, the feet should be spread about the width of the shoulders with one foot dropped back slightly. The body should be bent at the knees and at the waist so that as the blow is delivered the muscles of the legs and back as well as those of the shoulders and arm may be used in attacking the opponent.

If a player is in a proper hitting position, he will be able to deliver a forceful blow. As he hits, he must follow through the area of contact. With the proper follow-through, he will drive his opponent back and literally obliterate him. The importance of the follow-through has been emphasized over and over again in such games as golf or tennis. It is just as vital to a football player.

To effectively teach any subject to intelligent people, it is important that a student understand *why* he will do something in a certain manner. If he knows *why* he is doing it, the next step—*what* he is to do—becomes meaningful to him. When he has been told *why* he is to do something in a certain manner—and then is told *what* he is to do—he is told *how* to do it. In teaching linemen, this progression should always be followed. Intelligent people will learn rapidly if they understand the WHY, WHAT, and HOW of the technique to be used.

CHAPTER TWO

Basic Line Drills

Basically, there are four types of football drills for linemen. There are agility drills, reaction drills, conditioning drills and drills to create a situation the players will face in a game. Why you are doing a drill is most important, and you should decide what you are trying to accomplish. Is the drill an agility drill, reaction drill or a conditioning drill?

Most drills can be conditioning drills if the time limit is extended, or the number of reactions is increased. A drill that exceeds five or six seconds, or that has more than four or five reactions ceases to be an agility or reaction drill and becomes a conditioning drill.

What Makes a Good Drill

There are four fundamental requirements that make good drills as opposed to bad drills. A drill must have more than one reaction. There is no play in football where you have just one reaction. For example, if you are on defense, you have to attack the offensive man and control him. You have to ignore the fake, locate the ball, move to the ball and make the tackle. It is a series of reactions and every play in football is the same way. Drills where you have just one reaction are not good drills. Drills must have at least two reactions to be considered good drills.

Importance of Running

Since running is one of the basic fundamentals of football,

players must learn to run well. Just to get out and run becomes pretty old and becomes a drudgery. Therefore, it is necessary to have a considerable amount of running in drills and not have the players consciously realize they are doing it. Actually, they realize it without any question, but if the players are doing uninteresting running, such as sprints or running laps around the field, it gets very tiresome. Drills, in which running is secondary and not the primary reason for the drills, are much better to teach the players to run well than to have the players line up and just do the same type of running.

Football practice is tough by any standard, and if drills can become fun by being competitive, the execution of the drills will be better. Competitive drills make the best type of drills. Although, at times, it is hard to achieve, a drill should be made to be fun if it is at all possible to do so.

Vary Your Drills

The last important requirement for having successful drills is to have a variety of drills to accomplish the same fundamentals or techniques. It is not good to get involved in a practice session where the players know that at a certain time and for a certain number of minutes, they are going to do the same old drill. Practice is routine at best. If you have a variety of drills so that you can do one drill one day and another drill the next, both of which are going to develop the same techniques, the players will learn a little better. They will learn better because they will be a little fresher mentally and there is a little more imagination involved in doing something that is new. It is difficult to be enthusiastic doing something old.

The offensive starting count is most important. When possible, drills should be started on your starting count and stopped on a whistle. This method of starting and stopping drills will help the players become acclimated to game conditions.

A football field marked off with three rows of five yard squares along the sidelines *(Illustration #1)* will eliminate loss of practice time in setting up drills. The squares will almost enable you to have proper spacing, which is most important for specific drills.

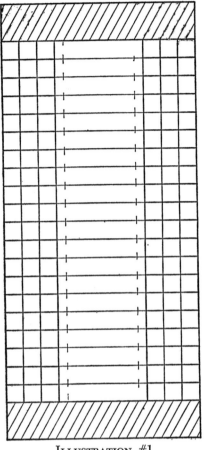

ILLUSTRATION #1.

Hit or Get Hit

Hit or get hit—football is a game of contact and one is either doing the hitting or is getting hit. A player who is not in a hitting position when he is within three (3) yards of contact will not be the player doing the hitting.

The Hitting Position

The hitting position will vary with the individual players. It is a position very much like that of a boxer's stance with a slightly greater bend at the knees. The arms are in a position to deliver a blow with either forearm (forearm-lift) or both hands (hand shiver) rather than with either fist. The delivering of a blow should be able to be made without making any unnecessary adjusting movement of the body.

The development of body control, agility and the ability to react with accuracy is as important as the development of offensive and defensive fundamentals. Without these required skills, players will not be able to execute the offensive and defensive fundamentals. The following drills are designed to develop these required skills of a football player:

1. QUARTER EAGLE DRILL. This drill places an emphasis on maintaining good body balance and the ability to move quickly. The action in this drill will also stretch the quadricep muscles (thigh) and hamstring muscles (back of leg) which will help the player be more agile.

In setting up this drill, the players line up five yards apart in two or three rows depending on the number of players participating in the drill *(Illustration #2)*. The coach places himself in a position in front of the players so that he will be able to see all of the players doing the drill.

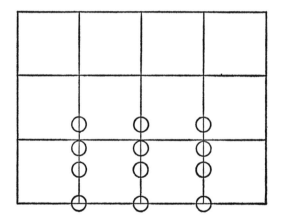

 COACH

ILLUSTRATION #2.

On the command "Ready", the first man in each row assumes the stance by placing his feet as wide as his shoulders. His feet should be parallel and flat on the ground. He should have a good bend at the knees so that his thighs are slightly above being parallel to the ground. His head should be up and his arms should be in a position from which the player may use a forearm-lift with either arm. On the command of "Hike", by the coach (always start a drill with your starting count when possible), the players hop in place executing quarter turns keeping their original base to maintain good balance. The number of quarter turns will vary with the individual player during the given amount of time of not more than five or six seconds. Stop the drill on a whistle. The more agile a player becomes, the more quarter turns he will be able to execute during the allotted time. Each man should do the drill three or four times.

2. SOMERSAULT DRILL. During a football game at sometime or another, players are blocked off their feet. It is necessary for a player to form the habit of recovery to his feet, gain his equilibrium while assuming the hitting position. In this drill, rather than blocking the player off his feet, the player puts himself on the ground by executing a somersault. At the completion of the somersault, he must regain his equilibrium as he assumes the hitting position.

Most athletes when practicing will always work on the fundamentals which they do well rather than those they do poorly. Since most people are right-handed, it is more difficult for them to use their left arm as effectively as their right. This makes it necessary to have drills in which the player must use his left forearm to do the hitting he will have to use it during a game. This can be done in the somersault drill by having the players use their left forearm two or three times to each right forearm.

The somersault drill is set up in the following manner (*Illustration #3*). The players line up in two rows five yards apart with two (2) men out in front five yards facing the men in the two rows. The coach places himself behind the two men in front and will tell them which forearm to use. Depending on which forearm they will use, the two men adjust slightly to the left or to the right; to the right when using the left forearm and to the left when using the right forearm. (The left forearm should be used two or three times more than the right forearm.)

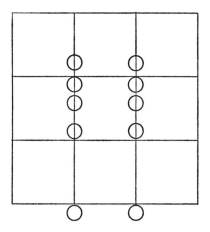

● *COACH*

ILLUSTRATION #3.

On the command of "Ready", the first man in each row and the two men in front assume a hitting position. On the command of "Hike", the first man in each row executes a somersault, gains his equilibrium and assumes a hitting position. The man in front starts moving forward and attacks the man doing the somersault with a forearm-lift. The man doing the somersault also uses a forearm-lift.

The men are five yards apart to give the man doing the somersault an opportunity to regain his balance and get into a hitting position before the man in front can attack him. This depends on the speed and agility of the man doing the somersault. When first doing this drill, the man doing the somersaults is usually defeated. This is not always the case after the men doing the somersaults realize why they are doing the drill. (To form a habit of regaining their feet and assuming a hitting position as quickly as possible after being blocked off their feet.) This drill is continued by having the two men who did the somersault assume their positions out in front. The two who were out in front go to the end of their respective rows. Each man should do three or four somersaults having to use his left forearm more times than his right.

3. WAVE DRILLS. Football is a game of movement. Players

never do anything from their original position They must move from one location to another quickly and accurately. Speed and accuracy in their movement are essential for success.

These drills emphasize changing directions frequently while reacting to the movement of the hands of the coach. Both wave drills can become conditioning drills if the number of reactions is extended. However, the purpose of the drills is to develop speed of reaction and accuracy of movement. The players should not change direction more than four or five times.

The wave drills are set up by having three rows of players five yards apart facing the coach who is ten yards in front of them (Illustration #4). The first wave drill is executed by the players in an upright stance. In this drill, the players will move only to their right or left. On the command of "Ready", the first player in each row assumes a position from which he can react without making any false or unnecessary movement. Reacting to the hand signals given by the coach, the player moves as fast as possible in the direction indicated, keeping his eyes on the coach as he moves. The players must turn and run in the direction indicated by the coach. To change directions, the player must stop on the foot opposite to the direction he must move. (Changing directions to the left, he must stop on his right foot.) He must change his weight to this foot so that he can push off with it, gaining as much ground as possible with the other foot in the direction he is moving. The players should not run more than three or four steps before the coach changes their direction. After four or five changes of direction, the coach should drop his hands indicating that the first three men have completed their drill. They then go to the end of their respective rows and the next three men move up. Each man should have three or four turns.

The second wave drill is set up in the same manner except that the players are in an all-four stance. Their hands should be slightly out in front of them with their feet well up in under them. (They assume this stance on the command "Ready"). In this drill, the players will move in all four directions, forward and backward as well as to their right and left. When moving right or left, their body should remain perpendicular. This is done by moving the hands as well as the feet in the direction they are moving. Keeping their feet well up under their bodies must be stressed.

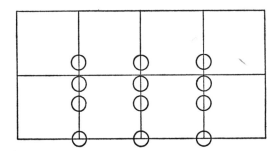

COACH

ILLUSTRATION #4.

After completing four or five reactions, the coach raises his arms indicating to the players to sprint five yards forward and that completes their turn. They should return to the end of their respective rows and the next three men move up. Each man should have three or four turns.

4. COMBINATION SOMERSAULT AND WAVE DRILL. One of the four fundamental requirements to make a good drill is to have more than one reaction in a drill. This is accomplished in the somersault-wave drill.

The drill is set up and executed in the same manner as the somersault drill. After the hitting has been done, the players who did the somersault must execute the wave drill in the same manner as the wave drill is done from the up-right position. Not more than three reactions should be used in this drill.

5. TRIANGLE DRILL. To execute a forearm-lift properly, the player must take a short, powerful step with the foot corresponding to the arm he is using; left foot with a left forearm, right foot with a right forearm. This drill emphasizes this, as well as reacting to the movement of the two men.

The two men line up 12 to 18 inches apart facing the third man. The third man should line up in the middle of the two men approximately 2 feet from them. Contact should be able to be made with each man taking one step. This drill can be executed with three groups of three men. *(Illustration #5).* The two men in each group are facing the coach who is 10 yards away in a position all six men can see him. The coach has his arms extended straight up so that he can give arm signals to them. On the command of "Ready", all men assume the hitting position. The coach then indicates which man of the two he wants to attack the man in front by simply moving his left or right arm. (This is another drill where the coach can control the number of left forearm-lifts used.) The man out in front must react to the man using the proper forearm-lift and stepping with the proper foot. After contact has been made, each man takes a step back and the coach gives another arm signal. The coach can have the same man do the attacking two or three times in succession. After four or five reactions, the three men rotate. Each man should be out in front three or four times before completing the drill.

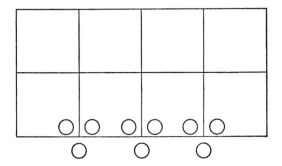

 COACH

ILLUSTRATION #5.

6. CIRCLE DRILL. Body control as well as being able to react and hit are essential to be a good player. This drill stresses these as well as developing peripheral vision.

This drill is best executed with seven men, however, eight can be used effectively. One player is in the middle of a circle composed of six or seven men. The circle should be approximately 5 yards in diameter (*Illustration #6*). This places the men in the circle two to two and one-half yards from the man in the middle. This will enable the man in the middle to react to the men in the circle.

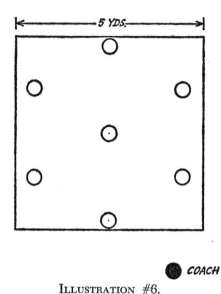

ILLUSTRATION #6.

On the command of "Ready", all men assume the hitting position. On the command of "Hike", the man in the middle of the circle starts moving his feet turning in place to the right and to the left. He must not turn in the same direction all of the time.

The men in the circle are instructed that when the man in the middle is facing him, he should not attack. The man on either side of him should do the attacking. The man in the middle will turn and use a forearm-lift on the man attacking him. Both men use the proper forearm-lift stepping with the proper foot at the time of contact. After contact has been made, the man from the circle moves back into place. Should both men on either side come in at the same time, the man whom the man in the middle does not turn to take on should have body control enough to stop continues to move rapidly until another man attacks him. and move back into place. After contact, the man in the middle

The man in the middle of the circle should be replaced every six or seven seconds. Stop the drill on a whistle. Should the man in the middle remain there longer, the drill will become a conditioning drill. This is not the purpose of this drill. Each man should have three or four turns in the middle of the circle.

7. SLED DRILLS (*Two Man Sled*).

a. *Hit, Hit, Hit Drill*—This drill is considered a good drill because it has more than one reaction. It also places emphasis on quickness as well as the proper executions of the forearm-lift.

This drill is set up with two rows of men in front of the sled and two men on either side and back of the sled. The first man is the outside man and the second man is the inside man (*Illustration #7*). On the command of "Ready," the first two men in front of the sled assume an all-four stance approximately a foot in front of the sled. On the command of "Hit", the men uncoil hitting the sled with their inside shoulder and forearm. After contact is made, they assume the all-four stance again ready for the next command of "Hit". The command of "Hit" is made three times. This is done rather rapidly which will make the players hustle to assume their stance.

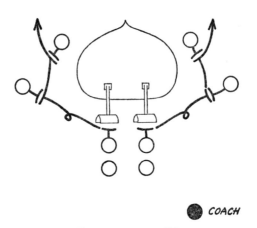

● *COACH*

ILLUSTRATION #7.

After the third hit, the players do a side-body roll-out regaining their feet and assuming a hitting position. The first man (outside) attacks him with a forearm-lift so that the player doing the drill must use his outside forearm. After contact is made, the second man (inside) attacks him with a forearm-lift from the inside so that the player must use his inside forearm. All three men use the forearm-lift. Body control should be stressed after the second man has made contact.

The men rotate by having the man who hit the sled take the inside position, the inside man takes the outside position, and the outside man goes to the end of the opposite row in front of the sled. This will enable the players to hit the sled with both shoulders and forearms. Each man should have three or four turns as the hit, hit, hit man.

b. *Belly Slammer*—Most offensive blocks are poorly executed because the offensive man has his head down and has a rounded back. This drill emphasizes players having their head up and an arched back. The use of the forearm as added blocking surface is also stressed.

The players line up in two rows in front of the sled. On the command of "Ready", the first two men assume their offensive stance with their shoulders approximately one foot from the sled. On the command of "Hike", both lunge, hitting the sled with their inside shoulder and forearm. Their heads are up and their backs arched. The sled will be moved back allowing the players to hit on their stomachs. The players will then scramble to their feet and sprint five yards.

This drill can be a competitive drill; which two men can block the sled the furthest? Which one of the two men can recover and sprint five yards the faster?

After the sprint, the two men return to the opposite row so that they will hit the sled with both shoulders. The next two men move up and the action is continued. Each man should have three or four turns.

c. *Drive the Sled*—Most poor offensive blockers take two steps and then go to the ground. By using the two-man sled, the players must be able to keep their feet moving to keep contact with the sled.

This drill forms a good habit of staying on your feet when blocking. It also helps their agility as well as develops their leg drive.

The players form two rows in front of the sled. On the command of "Ready", the first two men assume an offensive stance. The distance from his sled will depend on whether or not you want them to take one or two steps before making contact.

On the command of "Hike", the men move forward hitting the sled with their inside shoulder, using the forearm to increase their blocking surface. Their heads are up and their backs are arched. They continue to drive the sled by moving their feet rapidly gaining ground with each step. The ideal distance for them to drive the sled is 10 yards. Stop them on a whistle. The men return to the opposite row so that they will be hitting the sled with either shoulder. Each man should drive the sled three or four times.

The drills discussed in this chapter are primarily agility and reaction drills. Most of them can be conditioning drills if the time or number of reactions are extended.

CHAPTER THREE

Selecting of Personnel

No phase of coaching is more important or as difficult than the proper selection of players for positions at which they are best suited and will perform most effectively. This cannot be accomplished until the coaching staff has been able to select the best twenty-two football players on their squad.

There is no doubt in our minds that defense is the most important single phase of the game. If your opponent can be held scoreless, they cannot defeat you.

Since it is also our belief that it is more difficult to play defense than offense, these twenty-two players will be selected on their defensive ability and play.

In analyzing why it is more difficult to play defense than offense, the offensive linemen know where the play is going, when the ball will be snapped and whom they are going to block.

A defensive lineman does not know where the play is going, when the ball will be snapped and does not know who will block him. When the play is directed at a defensive lineman, he doesn't know the type of play it will be, he may be trapped, double teamed, cross blocked or isolated and blocked by a halfback. He must move on the snap of the ball and ward off offensive blockers while protecting his territory.

If the ball does not come in his area, he must locate it, react to other blockers while pursuing it and must be able to tackle the ball-carrier when he gets to him. On one offensive play, a defensive lineman will make at least three or four reactions while the offensive man has just one assignment.

Because defense is more difficult to play, defensive personnel should be organized so that the same fundamentals for most men remain the same on a variety of defensive alignments. This will simplify defensive assignments and minimize the chance of error.

There are three categories of personnel within the forcing unit:

1. Defensive linemen
2. Defensive linebackers
3. Defensive ends

When a 6:2:2:1 alignment is used, the defensive ends are, for the most part, included in the containing unit. They become part of the forcing unit only when they are included in a stunt or when an eight man rush is used. By using an end as the corner man on a 5:4:2 defense, he becomes a part of the secondary and is always in the containing portion of the defense. Since he has already played in the containing unit of a defense as a defensive end, he will already know some of the basic fundamentals of the play of the containing unit. He will now have only a minimum of other basic fundamentals to learn and be able to play as a corner man.

With the exception of this man and the other end, who must now play as a lineman, none of the other players on the forcing unit need to adjust or learn to execute any other basic defensive fundamentals. The other end, having played as a lineman, when stunting would have a minimum of basic defensive fundamentals to learn and be able to execute to play as a lineman.

There are teams that use the fullbacks as a corner man on the 5:4:2 alignment and as a linebacker on a 6:2:2:1 defensive alignment with a great deal of success.

However, by using this placement of personnel, the fullback must learn all the basic fundamentals for two positions, one in the containing unit and one in the forcing unit. Both defensive ends must learn the basic fundamentals for two positions, that of the end in the containing unit and that of a lineman in the forcing unit. One lineman must learn the basic fundamentals of a lineman and a linebacker when the odd defensive alignment with two linebackers is employed.

The chance of a defensive error is greater when defensive players must adjust from one position in one unit to another position in the other unit, or even from one position to another in the same unit which has different basic fundamentals.

It is the opinion of the author that the fewer fundamentals an individual has to master, the more effectively he will be able to play without errors. This being the case, by using the left defensive end as a corner man on a box defensive alignment, you have reduced to the absolute minimum the number of men who must adjust from one position to another as the alignment changes. This means that more men have less basic fundamentals to master and there is less possibility of defensive errors. Defensive errors will result into touchdowns which will defeat you.

Although defensive ability is primary, the offensive positions must also be taken into consideration. The split "T" formation requires a fullback who is a good open field blocker. He does not need to have speed nor be an outstanding ball carrier. To be an effective blocker and be able to maintain the pace during a 60 minute game, he must possess good size.

A player able to play fullback on offense would not likely have the qualifications of a secondary defensive man in the containing unit. He would more likely have the requirements of a linebacker in the forcing unit. He must, however, be able to play as a linebacker before he is considered as an offensive fullback possibility.

We had an outstanding example of this in 1954 in Jerry Tubbs. Jerry was an All-State center in high school. He played at that position as a freshman and was an outstanding college prospect. Having an excellent linebacker in Kurt Burris at center and being in need of a good linebacker at fullback, Jerry was changed to that position. He was not considered a great offensive fullback, but was an outstanding linebacker. His junior year, we discovered another fine linebacker in Billy Pricer, who was able to perform as an offensive fullback. Jerry was moved back to center where he proved to be an All-American, defensively and offensively in his senior year.

The best defensive players are determined by their defensive play in drills which are set up to create situations which the players in each category will face under game conditions.

From our defensive requirements for the forcing unit, the players would be placed on offense as follows:

1. Linemen who can use a hand shiver effectively and have the ability to move, react and tackle, would be selected to play right guard.

2. Linemen who can use their left forearm more effectively and have the other defensive abilities would be selected to play either right tackle or right end. The players who best combine the ability to block with a talent to catch the ball would be placed at the end position.

3. Linemen able to execute the defensive requirements on the left side of the line would be placed at left guard or left tackle on offense. The players possessing the most speed would be selected for the left tackle position.

4. Players with the ability to play the corner positions would be placed at left end or right halfback. To be able to play the corner position, the players should possess speed and have aptitude for catching the ball. The men with fairly good size and the ability to block on the line of scrimmage would be placed at left end.

5. Men possessing the ability to be linebackers would be selected to play fullback or center, depending on their offensive abilities.

When selecting players, coaches must keep in mind the basic requirements for each position and attempt to place individual players in the position at which they will perform most effectively and thereby will be able to make their maximum contribution to the team effort.

The same is true about offense as defense, the fewer offensive techniques a player must master, the more effectively he will be able to play without making errors.

There are times when individual players will be more effective at one position than another, but the lack of personnel for a position may necessitate switching a man to another position at which he is less effective. However, he would be more effective at the new position than any other player and thereby improve the overall team strength.

The selection and proper placement of personnel cannot be accomplished after one practice nor probably not even after one week of practice. The re-alignment of personnel is a continuing process until the best twenty-two players on the squad are lined up on the first two teams with the best eleven on the starting lineup.

CHAPTER FOUR

Offensive Nomenclature

In sciences such as mathematics, chemistry and physics, terms and symbols have precise meanings. These terms and symbols mean the same thing to everyone. In football, there are no universal terms which mean the same thing. Different coaching staffs use different terminology to describe exactly the same stance or play.

If players are to learn your football easily and correctly, it is necessary that they exactly know and understand every coaching phrase you use. It is most important that every coach on the staff uses the same nomenclature so as not to confuse the players. The players must know precisely what you mean when you use a particular term:

Terms to Describe Fundamental Offensive Techniques

1. FIRE OUT—Getting off the line of scrimmage at full speed *with* the starting count.
2. ONE-ON-ONE—A straight shoulder block (left or right) where one offensive man blocks one defensive man.
3. REVERSE SHOULDER—A block where the offensive man fakes the One-on-One Block by driving his head past his opponent on the side *away* from the hole.
4. SIDE-BODY BLOCK—Block used when the defensive man has the advantage on the offensive man.
5. SCRAMBLE BLOCK—Block used to cut off pursuit.

25

6. REVERSE-BODY BLOCK—Block used when the offensive man has the advantage on the defensive man.

7. CROSS-BODY BLOCK—Block used downfield on secondary man.

8. RUNNING SHOULDER BLOCK—Block used downfield on secondary men.

9. NEAR FOOT

   a. On a One-on-One Block, the foot closer to the defensive man you are blocking.

   b. The foot next to the man with whom you are blocking when double-teaming or picking up a Cross Charge.

10. STEP FOR POSITION—A lineman stepping laterally instead of straight at his opponent. This is the *worst mistake* an offensive lineman can make.

11. OPPONENT SHOOTS GAP—If an offensive lineman steps for position, his opponent, if slanting, will penetrate across the line of scrimmage and stop the play.

12. TAKE HIM SMART WAY—When a defensive lineman loops or slants (slanting defense) instead of charging straight ahead, the blocker must take him in the direction he is giving. When he is on the off-side and moves away from the play, the offensive lineman should let him go and move downfield ahead of the ball carrier.

13. INFLUENCE BLOCK—The fake of an aggressive block by an offensive lineman which causes the defensive lineman to penetrate and leave himself vulnerable to trap.

14. POSITION BLOCK—Block used on passes, kick protection, etc., where the offensive lineman does not attempt to move the defensive player, but keeps him from penetrating to a particular area.

15. UTILITY BLOCKER—Any man who does not have a specific blocking assignment and who takes the first opponent who gets away from his original blocker.

16. POSITION OF DEFENSIVE MAN

   a. Linemen—A defensive man who lines up within one yard and a half of the line of scrimmage.

b. Linebackers—Any man who lines up between a yard and an half to four yards from the line of scrimmage.

Any man who is in the area of a yard and an half, and it is questionable as to whether he is a lineman or a linebacker, his stance will be the determining factor. If he is in a three point stance, he will be considered a lineman. Should he be in an upright stance, he would be considered a linebacker.

c. Secondary Men—Any man who lines up further than four yards from the line of scrimmage.

17. DEFENSIVE SETS—The alignments used by the opponents playing in the immediate area of an offensive lineman.

18. EXPERIMENT—Adjustments in splits by offensive linemen to determine their most advantageous position. This is the most important single factor in intelligent offensive line play for split "T" linemen.

19. BE UP ON BALL—Each offensive lineman must take his position on the line of scrimmage, not behind it.

20. SPLITS—The variations in lateral spacing between offensive linemen.

21. SPREAD THE DEFENSE—The reason offensive linemen split.

22. BLOCKING ANGLE—An alignment taken by the defensive linemen which gives the offensive linemen position to block the opponent in or out.

23. CROSS CHARGE SITUATION—Whenever a defensive lineman and a linebacker take their position close enough to each other so that they could Cross Charge. The lineman may shoot the gap one way while the linebacker shoots to the opposite side.

24. STUNT POSITION—Whenever the defensive man is lined up a foot or more off the line of scrimmage, he is in position to loop or slant. Offensive linemen must recognize this position and anticipate the possible stunt charge.

25. "C" BLOCKING—The signal between the tackle and the end to exchange blocking assignments.

26. "B" BLOCKING—The signal between the guard and the tackle to exchange blocking assignments.

27. "A" BLOCKING—The signal between the center and the off-side guard to exchange blocking assignments.

28. "O" BLOCKING—The signal between the center and the on-side guard to exchange blocking assignments.

29. ON-SIDE—The side to which the play will be directed.

30. OFF-SIDE—The side away from the point of attack.

31. DOUBLE TEAM BLOCK (POST AND DRIVER)—Block used by two offensive linemen to block one defensive lineman.

32. COVERAGE—Movement by the offensive line laterally to the side of a forward pass so that they will be in a position to tackle an opponent should the pass be intercepted.

33. DOWNFIELD BLOCKING ANGLE—When going downfield to block, move on a course which will place you in position between the defensive players and the ball carrier as quickly as possible.

CHAPTER FIVE

Offensive Fundamentals

Blocking is the most important element in offensive football. At least 90 per cent of all offensive action or energy in football is used in blocking.

If an offensive play is to be successful, the offensive line must knock their opponents back off the line of scrimmage. To accomplish this, they must line up on the ball. Tackles and ends must be particularly conscious of being up on the ball. This will enable the entire offensive line to get across the line of scrimmage with their first step.

The entire offensive line must get off with the starting count. One slow starter will allow a defensive man to penetrate and ruin the play. The offensive line must move their feet gaining ground forward. This will enable the ball carrier to gain ground.

The two phases in all blocking are the approach and the block itself. The approach involves the stance, the moving into position where the block is to be applied, the contact, and the body position of the blocker. The block itself involves the delivering of a sharp blow to break the opponent's charge and drive him back by following through aggressively.

In making a block, the offensive lineman must attack from a good stance. He must get contact as quickly as possible and maintain contact with aggressivness until he has succeeded in keeping his opponent from tackling the ball carrier.

Most offensive blocking failures are caused by one of the following:

    1. The offensive man tipping off what he is going to do.

2. Failing to move quickly to the point of the block.
3. Letting his feet trail rather than having them under him with a good base giving him balance in all directions.
4. Forgetting to keep moving with his opponent.
5. Not knowing what to do.

Stance. In line play, the most important single fundamenal is the stance. Usually, a lineman will have failed or succeeded in carrying out his assignment with his first two or three steps. The defensive man who will attack the offensive lineman is only thirteen inches away from him. If the stance of the offensive lineman is not good, he is handicapped materially since there is not time enough for him to adjust and get in a good position before he makes contact.

A lineman in taking his stance should have his feet apart about the width of his shoulders. Either foot of the lineman may be dropped back slightly, but not further than the heel of the opposite foot. This will enable the lineman to step with either foot first when it is necessary to do so.

The feet should be perpendicular to the line of scrimmage. The heels should be slightly off the ground. The knees should be apart the same width as the feet. The hand corresponding with the rear foot should be placed on the ground about 6 to 8 inches in front of the corresponding shoulder and slightly inside of the corresponding foot. This will enable the lineman to have his shoulders parallel to the ground and his feet well up under him, which is essential in having a good stance. The weight placed on the hand should be equal to the weight placed on the feet.

The back should be parallel to the ground, head up with a firm neck and the eyes looking straight down the field. The wrist of the other arm should be placed slightly above the knee which will put the arm in an advantageous position to be used as added blocking surface when blocking with the corresponding shoulder. This stance is not a comfortable one, but one from which the lineman can move forward quickly, deliver a blow, and have good balance.

The main difference between this stance used by Split "T" linemen and the stance used by linemen for other offensive formations is the hand position on the ground and the amount of weight placed on it. When a lineman is required to pull out of the line to lead interference, to trap, and for pass protection, the hand on the ground is not placed as far out in front of the shoulder and little or no weight is placed on the hand. The head and shoulders may be slightly higher than the buttocks.

Start. From any offensive stance, a lineman must be able to step off with either foot first. Normally, the first step will be taken by the rear foot and it can be from 12 to 18 inches long. However, if the defensive man is playing in the gap to either side of the offensive man, the first step should be taken with the rear foot.

Should there be a cross-charge situation in the area of two offensive linemen, both offensive linemen should step with their *near* foot (the near foot is the foot next to the offensive man with whom you are blocking). Their first step should not be more than 6 inches. This will enable them to pick up the two defensive men should they cross-charge.

Assignments of blockers will vary, but they will always fall into one of the following classifications:

1. On-Side
   A. Hole Openers—the men whose job it is to open the hole between two defensive linemen (could be a man from the off-side trap blocker).
   B. Check Blockers—the men engaged in preventing a lineman from pursuing.
2. Off-Side Blockers.
   A. Check Blockers—the men engaged in preventing a lineman from pursuing.
   B. Secondary Blockers—the men who are assigned to block definite men in the secondary.
3. Either side
   A. Lead Men—the men who are running in a path preceeding the ball carrier.
   B. Trap Blocker—a man whose job it is to block one of the defensive men at the point of attack.

The types and techniques of offensive blocks used by linemen are as follows:

1. POST AND DRIVER. A double team block with one lineman

being the post blocker and another lineman being the driver. The primary objective of the post blocker is to stop the charge of the defensive man. The post blocker moves out from his stance with a short, driving step with the foot next to the drive blocker. The corresponding shoulder should be directed at the midsection of the defensive man. He does not follow through his block as his basic thought is to break the charge of the defensive man and not to drive him back off the line of scrimmage.

The second objective of the post blocker is to keep the defensive man from going between the driver and himself. As he feels pressure from the driver, the post blocker maneuvers his feet so that his hip is as close as possible to the driver. This is done by the post blocker taking faster and longer driving steps with the foot next to the driver. This will permit the driver to move the defensive man down the line of scrimmage to create a lateral opening and keep the defensive man away from the path of the ball carrier.

The first objective of the driver is not to allow the defensive man to slant charge between the post blocker and himself. The drive blocker must move out of his stance with a longer driving step directed at the defensive man with the foot next to the post blocker. The corresponding shoulder should be in a position that will permit him to drive the defensive man down the line of scrimmage.

The second objective of the driver is not to allow the defensive man to slide off his block away from the line of scrimmage. This is done by the driver maneuvering his feet so that his outside foot is beyond the defensive man.

2. SHOULDER BLOCKS.

a. *Straight shoulder blocks*—The basic block used by offensive linemen is the one-on-one straight shoulder block. When executing this block, the offensive lineman moves out from his stance with powerful steps, moving his feet rapidly and gaining ground forward.

The forehead should be directed at the chin of the defensive man. As the defensive man raises up, the head of the offensive man should continue straight ahead driving at the stomach of the defensive man. Just before making contact, or after making contact with the forehead, the offensive man should slide his head by the defensive man's hip on the proper side (the head should slide by to the right when blocking with the left shoulder and to the left when using the right shoulder).

The offensive man should hit sharply with his shoulder and upper arm, with the arm bent at the elbow, and with his fist on his chest. The forearm should be parallel to the ground. The blocker should move his other arm in a normal running motion to maintain good balance. As contact is made with the shoulder, the offensive lineman should maneuver his feet so that the foot corresponding to the hitting shoulder will be in the center of the defensive man's stance and the other foot on the outside and beyond the defensive man. The blocker should keep his feet moving and driving forward maintaining the same foot position. The foot position can be described as a double team block; the foot in center of the defensive man being the post driver and the other foot as the drive blocker.

b. *Reverse shoulder block*—This block is used when the defensive lineman is keying and reacting to the head of the offensive man. A defensive lineman playing this type of defense will move laterally through the head of the offensive lineman. To execute this block, the offensive lineman moves out from his stance by taking a driving step with the foot opposite the shoulder with which he is blocking. His forehead should be directed slightly outside of the defensive man's hip while driving his shoulder into the midsection of his opponent.

As the defensive man moves laterally, the offensive man should maneuver his feet so that the foot opposite the shoulder with which he is blocking will be in the center of the defensive man's stance using it as the post blocker. The foot corresponding to the hitting shoulder should be used as the driver blocking the defensive man in the direction he is moving.

3. SCRAMBLE BLOCK. This block is used primarily to eliminate pursuit by a defensive lineman. However, it can be used at the point of attack as well as on linebackers. When using this block, the offensive lineman moves out of his stance by taking a slight cross-over step with the foot corresponding to the shoulder with which the block is to be made. The corresponding shoulder should

be directed at the far knee of the defensive lineman The offensive lineman should be moving across the line of scrimmage on all fours attempting to drive his shoulder through the knee, knocking the leg from under the defensive man. Should this be accomplished, he will block the defensive man with his hip. Should he not be able to knock the leg from under the defensive man, he must keep contact with the defensive man with his shoulder. In either case, the offensive lineman must continue his movement on all fours.

4. SIDE BODY BLOCK. This block is used primarily on wide plays when the defensive man has the advantage on the offensive man.

On executing this block, the offensive man moves out of his stance by pivoting on his near foot and taking a long cross-over step with his far foot. The offensive man should be gaining ground across the line of scrimmage directing his head and shoulder outside of the defensive man's hip. The block should be made with the far hip of the offensive man. After taking the next step with the near foot, the offensive man should maneuver his feet so that the near foot is used as the driver and the far foot as the post. At the same time, the offensive man should go into an all four position, keeping contact with the defensive man by continuing his movement on all fours.

5. REVERSE BODY BLOCK. This block is used primarily on delayed plays such as reverses when the offensive lineman must block the defensive man for longer periods of time. It is used when the offensive man has a blocking angle on the defensive man. The offensive man moves out of his stance by taking a short, lateral step with his near foot so that it is in the middle of the defensive man's stance. This foot is used momentarily as the post to keep the defensive man from penetrating. The far shoulder of the offensive man should be directed slightly in front of the far hip of the defensive man. The second step should be a normal one directed at the defensive man. As the defensive man moves laterally with the first flow of the play, the offensive man should keep contact with him with the side of his body going into an all four position. As the defensive man reacts to the ball, the offensive man should maneuver his feet so that his near foot (the foot opposite the side with which he is blocking) becomes the driver and his far foot the post. He should block the defensive man

back toward the line of scrimmage and not allow him to slide off his block away from the line of scrimmage.

Downfield or Secondary Blocking. Whether a running attack is successful or not depends on how effectively the linebackers are being blocked. The vital factor in making long runs or break-away touchdowns is the blocking the ball carriers get downfield beyond the linebackers. However, this is a wasted effort unless you succeed in blocking the linebackers.

Off-side blockers must always use judgment in their blocking. They cannot use judgment unless they know the nature of the play (including whether it is a direct or deceptive play; in which direction the fake is; and how fast will the ball actually get to the line of scrimmage?)

Course of Blockers. Downfield blockers on scrimmage plays should always run as fast as necessary on a straight *shallow* course that will, at the earliest possible moment, enable him to cross the path of the ball carrier about a yard in front of him. He should always block the first man he contacts on this course. If he meets no one before getting to the ball carrier, he should either cross in front of him blocking the opponent coming in from the other side, turn downfield becoming a lead man or protect the ball carrier from the rear.

Downfield blockers are frequently delayed and cannot get off the line of scrimmage in time to get in front of the ball carrier. Should this happen, the downfield blockers should try to get as close as possible to the ball carrier. Frequently, he can still be an effective blocker and it will always put him in a position to do some good if there is a fumble.

Downfield blockers should not be concerned with which way they block the defensive secondary men. They should block them in the direction of which they are the surest. It is the responsibility of the ball carrier to adjust himself to the downfield blocks. Downfield blockers should always use a legal block and should never clip a man to block him.

There are a number of situations in football where every player except the man with the ball suddenly becomes downfield blockers. The basic principles are exactly the same as on running plays from scrimmage and the results are just as important.

This will occur upon the completion of a forward pass, an intercepted pass, or any other situation where suddenly a team finds itself in possession of the ball.

The two blocks used on linebackers are the running straight shoulder block and the cross body block. When executing these blocks, good position on the part of the offensive blocker in relation to the course of the ball carrier is most important.

When the offensive play is directed at a linebacker, the running straight shoulder block is used. The execution of which is the same as the straight shoulder block on the line of scrimmage. However, since the linebackers are in an upright position, the forehead of the offensive blocker should be directed at the numerals on the jersey of the defensive man rather than at his chin.

Should the offensive play be directed at a point away from the linebackers, the offensive blocker will use a cross body block attempting to eliminate the linebacker's pursuit.

To execute the cross body block, the offensive lineman must get his foot, opposite to the side with which he is blocking, beyond the defensive man. At the same time, he must get the corresponding arm and shoulder of the side with which he is blocking beyond and past the defensive man. He then must drive off his outside foot blocking the defensive man with his hip attempting to knock the defensive man off his feet.

Should the defensive man remain on his feet, the blocker should keep contact with him by maneuvering into an all four position occupying him so that he cannot pursue the ball carrier.

The cross body block is usually used in blocking the deep secondary men. However, the running shoulder block is used with a great deal of success when the blocker is in a position to execute it. The most important single fundamental of downfield blocking is the *course* which the downfield blocker runs.

Pulling Linemen. A pulling lineman may be assigned to trap, lead interference, take part in protecting the passer, to influence a defensive man, or even to carry the ball (the initial movement out of the line should be one complete action).

The two most popular methods of pulling out of the line are the pivot-out and the cross-over.

1. *Pivot Out*—To execute the pivot-out method, the lineman moves out of his stance by pivoting on his far foot while taking a

diagonally drop step with the near foot; gaining as much ground as possible in the direction he is moving. He then drives off with the far foot pushing off with the hand on the ground while swinging the other arm to aid in pivoting his body in the direction he is going. The body should be kept low and under control while pivoting and continuing on his course. The depth of the drop step will depend upon the requirements of the lineman's assignment. Should he be assigned to lead or influence, the step is generally shallow. If assigned to trap or take part in protecting the passer, the step is generally deeper. This type of pull-out has been found most satisfactory in our coaching experience.

2. *Crossover*—The cross-over method is executed by having the lineman in one motion pivot and drive off the near foot while crossing over with the far foot using the hand on the ground to aid the push-out. In this type of pull-out, it is important that the pivot be pronounced enough so that the cross-over step can be deep enough to clear the next lineman on the line of scrimmage.

PULLING TO TRAP. A trap block is actually the one-on-one straight shoulder block applied from a different position with the blocker having a blocking angle on the defensive man. The first two steps of an offensive lineman pulling to trap a defensive man should be automatic. He should pivot on his far foot while taking a *deep* lateral step with his near foot gaining as much ground as possible in the direction he is going.

His next step should be taken with his far foot down the line of scrimmage toward his opponent. This course will put the offensive man in a position to block a defensive man who does not charge across the line of scrimmage. While taking the first two steps, the offensive lineman must look at the defensive man he is going to block as the play of this man will determine the direction of his third step.

The third step should be directed so that at the time of contact, the blocker can drive his foot, corresponding to the hitting shoulder, in the center of the defensive man's stance. As the offensive man approaches contact, he should direct his head downfield between his opponent and the line of scrimmage driving his shoulder into the midsection of the defensive man. The foot opposite the hitting shoulder should be maneuvered beyond the defensive man. This will prevent the defensive man from sliding off the block away from the line of scrimmage to tackle the ball carrier. The blocker should continue to keep contact by moving his feet to maintain his foot position.

LEAD INTERFERENCE. The depth of the initial step as well as the course of the pulling lineman to lead interference will be determined by the type of the offensive play. If the play is a deep reverse on a wide sweep, the lineman would generally use a deep, drop step and his course would be deep in the backfield. Should the play be a faster hitting play such as an inside or off-tackle play, the pulling lineman would use a shallow, drop step and his course would be parallel to the line of scrimmage enabling him to get to the point of attack before the ball carrier.

On any type of play, the pulling lineman should be under control, ready to block the first opponent who appears in his path. As the pulling lineman approaches the point of attack and stars his turn upfield, he must stay low. This can be accomplished by having the pulling lineman touch the ground with his inside hand as he makes the turn. He must be in a position to use a shoulder block on a defensive man who is in the hole at the point of attack. Should he clear the point of attack without making contact, he then should continue to move with top controlled speed until he has the opportunity to block an opponent.

PULLING TO INFLUENCE. A lineman pulling to influence a defensive man would pull to the outside as though he were going to lead interference. Should the defensive man playing in front of him react to him and move to the outside with him, it would set up the defensive man to be blocked out by a trap blocker coming from the inside.

PULLING FOR PASS PROTECTION. The type of pass would determine the depth and direction of the initial step as well as the course of the pulling lineman. Should the pass be a drop-back, pocket-type pass, the pulling lineman would use a deep, drop step. His course would be one that would enable him to have an inside position on the defensive man he is assigned to block. This should force the defensive man to take the outside course which would keep him from rushing the passer. Should the pass be a running pass, the pulling lineman would use a drop step and take a course that would put him in a position to be able to carry out the requirements of his assignments.

PASS PROTECTION BLOCKS. Basically, there are two types of passes, the drop back pass and the play pass. The drop back pass is thrown from an area five to seven yards deep behind the center. In blocking for this type pass, the offensive lineman, since he is not attempting to drive the defensive lineman off the line of scrimmage, need not make an aggressive block on the snap of the ball. The primary objective of the lineman is to form a pocket around the passer and not allow him to be rushed from the inside.

1. To execute this type of protection, the offensive lineman will move out of his stance by taking a drop step with his outside foot attempting to make the defensive man take an outside course. Should the defensive man take the outside course, the offensive man would block him with his outside shoulder keeping his head between the defensive man and the passer. The defensive man's own momentum, if properly directed, will take him out of the passing area.

Should the defensive man fake to the outside and then take the inside course, the offensive man would take a drop step with his inside foot. He then should drive his head and outside shoulder in front of the defensive man and execute a side body block keeping his body between the defensive man and the passer.

2. A play pass is one when a pass is thrown after faking the start of a running play. The passing area will vary with different running fakes. Linemen must be fully aware of the various passing areas and adjust to their position blocks accordingly.

The pass protection block by the offensive linemen should start with the same initial movements as the running play from which the pass will be attempted. Aggressive contact with the defensive lineman will make him, and any secondary man keying the offensive linemen, think it is a running play. After contact is made, the offensive lineman would move in a position block placing himself between the defensive man and the area from which the pass will be thrown. From this position, the pass protector can maneuver the pass rusher away from the passing area.

After the running fake, should the passing area be behind the center, all offensive linemen would maneuver into an inside position block. Should the passing area be outside, the on-side linemen would move to an outside position block, and the off-side linemen would move to an inside position block.

By doing this, all the offensive linemen have placed themselves between the defensive linemen and the pass area.

PASS COVERAGE. To be able to protect the passer successfully, the offensive linemen must know the area from which the pass will be thrown. It is as vitally important that they also know the area to which the pass will be thrown. On all pass plays, the first objective of offensive linemen is to protect the passer. The second objective is to cover the pass in case of an interception. It is the responsibility of each offensive lineman to put himself in a position to tackle the interceptor. In order to do this, the offensive lineman must know the area to which the pass will be thrown so that each offensive lineman can take his proper angle of pursuit to make the tackle and avoid the long return of an intercepted pass.

CHAPTER SIX

Special Techniques

The "T" formation center, in addition to being able to execute the basic fundamentals and techniques of an offensive lineman, must be able to make the automatic exchange with the quarterback. He must also be able to make the long snapback on deep-punt formation.

Center Techniques

The offensive center rates special attention since he initiates every single offensive play. The offense has the advantage of knowing not only where the play is directed, but also when the ball will be snapped. However, if the center anticipates the starting count and passes the ball early, the defense will gain this advantage since they will charge on the snap of the ball. It is of paramount importance that the center does not anticipate the snap count and take away this advantage which the offensive linemen have over the defense.

This automatic exchange should be completed as quickly as possible. Most centers would like to make a soft, easy pass to avoid having the quarterback fumble it. A slow pass will enable the defensive lineman to outcharge the offense before the pass is completed. This necessitates the center to snap the ball fast, hard and accurately. In making the automatic exchange, the center should think of the snap as a lift rather than a throw. There should never be a fumble on the automatic exchange when executed properly.

There are several types of automatic exchanges between the center and the quarterback, which are executed succssfully most

41

of the time. The majority of these exchanges require the center to twist or lock his wrist most of the time, in an awkward manner.

Any motion done normally can be executed with more consistent accuracy. Our centers lift the ball with a normal motion which will cause the ball to turn slightly and keep the longitudinal axis of the ball approximately parallel to the ground. He simply bends his elbow and wrist normally, directing the ball at the right hand of the quarterback.

The quarterback places his right hand well up in under the center's crotch so that his index finger is in the middle of the crotch. The quarterback then applies pressure with his right hand enabling the center to feel his target. The left hand is then placed so that the thumbs are together forming a pocket for the ball.

A center should take his stance with his left foot dropped back to about the instep of his right foot. This will enable the center, as he makes the snap, to have a little more freedom of movement with his right arm. With his left foot dropped back, the center takes the same stance previously described for offensive linemen. His back is parallel to the ground, his shoulders square to the line of scrimmage, his head is up and his feet are well up in under him.

The ball is placed on the ground at arm's length with the laces of the ball facing the right sideline. The center grasps the front half of the ball with his right hand which is in a straight line with his forearm. His thumb is just slightly across the top seam of the ball and his fingers are spread and extended. He must have a firm grip being able to control the ball.

Our centers have the option of using either one or two hands on the ball. If he uses one hand, the point of the ball is placed in line with the right side of his neck. This will enable him to keep his stance squared with the line of scrimmage.

If both hands are used, the point of the ball will be placed exactly in line with the center's nose. The ball will be grasped exactly the same way with the right hand, while the left hand will be placed on the left side in position to guide the ball for a short distance as the snap is being made. The center must lift the ball with maximum speed and force as he charges out to make his block on the play.

To execute the long snapback on deep punt, the center may widen his base slightly. Other than that, his stance remains the same. The ball is placed on the ground well out in front of the center with the laces turned down. The ball is grasped with the right hand in the same manner which a forward passer would grip the ball. The right hand should be turned under the ball so that the hand will be as close to a 90 degree angle to the forearm as possible. This will enable the center to have a good wrist snap. This is the hand with which the ball is actually passed.

The left hand is placed on the top left side of the ball with the index finger parallel to the top seam of the ball. The left hand merely guides the ball. As the ball is snapped, both hands should follow through low. This type of follow-through eliminates the high pass over the quarterback's head.

It is always possible that a punter may field a low pass from center and still get the kick away. There is no possible chance of getting a punt away when the pass from center is over the kicker's head. Little or no weight should be placed on the ball. This will also cause the high pass. The center is actually making a forward pass between his legs with the aid of his left hand.

Since the center will have his head down when making the long snapback to the punter, he will be unable to block as well as he cannot see his opponent. As the snap is made, a drop step with either foot or both feet as he brings his head up will put him on even terms with the defensive man.

He now will be able to see him and will be able to execute his block. Should he not have an opponent to block, after dropping back, he then can release and cover the kick.

End Techniques

Offensive formations have different requirements that must be considered when selecting personnel to play certain positions. Should the offensive formation be primarily a passing formation, the coaches will consider only speed and ability to catch the ball when selecting their ends. The Spit "T" Formation is primarily a running offense which necessitates having players who can block and also have an aptitude for catching the ball. In either case, ends have to learn the technique of pass receiving.

Basically, pass receiving is divided into three phases. These are (1) getting downfield, (2) running the proper course and (3) catching the ball.

There are several ways to get downfield. Probably, the most successful one is to drive at the defensive man exactly as you would if you were blocking him. The defensive man will usually try to avoid being blocked by the end which makes it easy for him to release and go downfield. This may also help the pass play, should the secondary be keying the end for a pass or run.

The end may make a feint with his head and shoulders in one direction to draw the defensive man out of position, then drive by him on the opposite side. The end must not raise up; he must stay low using his elbows to ward off the defensive charge of any-one who is trying to delay him.

The end may pick out a spot 18 inches to one side and 1½ yards behind the defensive man. As the ball is snapped, he executes a shoot-out by making a low dive at the spot bringing his feet well up under him. This enables him to be in a good position to come up running and continue downfield with a minimum delay.

The end will find it easier to get out on a pass if he widens his split between himself and his tackle. However, he cannot take this position only on a pass play as the defense will recognize it and will play for a pass play.

Teams that depend on the passing game to maintain possession of the ball depend on receivers with speed and the ability to fake as well as catching the ball. This type of offense usually employs flankers and men in motion to isolate a defender with a large area to cover. They then send their best receivers into that area to outmaneuver the one defensive man. The success of the pass play depends on the ability of the receiver. He should be excep-tionally good at faking, have superior speed and a good pair of hands.

The end may use the following fakes to outmaneuver the defender:

1. *Feint and Break*—The receiver feints one way with his head and shoulders and breaks in the opposite direction.

2. *Hook*—The end starts downfield full speed as though he were going deep and at a designated spot, usually 8 to 10

yards deep. He stops quickly by planting his outside foot. He then pivots back toward the passer ready to receive the ball.

3. *Hook and Slide*—Same maneuver as above with the receiver moving to the outside as the defender covers him.

4. *Hook and Go*—The receiver executes the hook and then breaks behind the defender.

A team employing an offense such as the split "T" formation, which uses the running game to maintain possession of the ball, will depend on play passes with definite patterns as their passing attack. On this type of pass, the offensive team will attempt to get a receiver open by drawing the defense out of position by a running fake or decoy.

The receiver must run his route just as it has been designed and he will have to time his cut into the designated area just as it clears. Exceptional speed and the ability to fake are not as essential as good judgment and good timing on the part of the receiver. He still must be able to catch the ball.

Catching the Ball

When a receiver has cleared the line of scrimmage and is in the area of the pass, he must carry his arms fairly high and keep the upper part of his body relaxed. After the ball is in the air, he must judge immediately where you can catch it at its highest point in flight. If the pass is short, he must come back to catch it. He should not wait until it comes to him.

A receiver cannot run as fast with his arms outstretched. Therefore, he should not reach for the ball until the last possible moment. He must keep his eyes on the ball. He should never take his eyes off the ball until it is firmly in his hands. He must fight hard for the ball. A tie ball belongs to the offensive man. If he cannot catch the ball, he should make sure it is not intercepted.

Kicking Assignments and Responsibilities

The kick-off and the kick, after a safety has been scored, are the only kick plays that offensive linemen do not need to protect the kicker. On all other kicks, punts, quick kicks, field goals, and point after touchdowns the linemen must protect the kicker.

The responsibilities of the offensive linemen on kick plays are:

1. Protect the kicker.

2. Cover the kick so effectively that there will be no return. The center is responsible for the snap either to the kicker or ball holder on all kick plays.

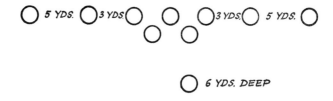

SPREAD PUNT FORMATION ILLUSTRATION #1.

Splits and Blocking Assignments

Center: Snap the ball to the kicker. Block the man over you. If there is no man over you, go downfield. If there is a cross-charge possibility in your area, use zone blocking.

Guards: Split the width of one man from the center. Block the man over you or the first man to the outside. If there are three defensive men in your area, call "help" to the tackle. If there is a three-man cross-charge possibility in your area, call "help" to your tackle; use zone blocking.

Tackle: Split three yards from your guard. Block the man over you or the first man to your outside. If the guard calls for help, move in no closer than a yard from your guard. Block the first man outside your guard. If there is a cross-charge possibility, block zone. If you had a man to block, call "help" to your end.

Ends: Split five yards from your tackle. Block the man over you or the first man to the outside. If your tackle calls for help, move in no closer than a yard from your tackle and block the first man outside your tackle.

The up backs are responsible for the man in the gap between the center and guard. If there is no one in the gap, block the first man in the gap outside the guard. The fullback lines up six yards deep and is responsible for keeping the kicking area clear. He will block the first man approaching the area. The front nine men will block for one and a half counts before releasing downfield to cover the kick.

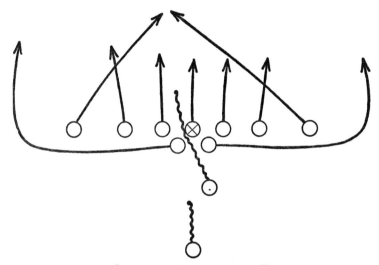

COVERAGE ILLUSTRATION #2.

The ends are responsible for forcing the ball carrier. They go downfield to the ball and make the tackle from the outside in. Should they miss the tackle, the ball carrier must go inside them.

The other linemen, depending on their splits, fan out accordingly and cover the kick full speed. If the defense causes them to cut their splits, they should fan out more. The two up backs, after blocking, run straight toward the sidelines. When they are ten yards from the sideline, they turn downfield. They are the leverage men and must turn the ball carrier in.

The fullback covers ¾ speed and is the first safety man. The kicker lines up 13 yards deep and after he kicks the ball covers

½ speed He is the safety man. Actually, the coverage turns into a 7:1:2:1 defensive alignment.

TIGHT PUNT FORMATION ILLUSTRATION #3.

Assignments—Protection

Right End: Go downfield on pass of ball. Cover kick as soon as possible.

Left End: Split out three yards if there is only one man between you and your tackle. If there are two men between you and your tackle, move in close enough to block the outside man with a sharp shoulder block before going downfield.

Center: Pass the ball. Take a quick short step back with either foot. Take a blocking position and hold ground until the ball is kicked.

Tackles and Guards: Take a quick short step back with their outside foot. You are responsible for your inside. You may lean to the outside to help, but you must be ready to protect the inside whenever there is a shooting linebacker.

#1 and #2 Backs: Line up 1½ yards behind their tackle, splitting his outside leg. Step up with his inside foot. You are responsible for the territory to your inside. Do not be pulled out of position by a man charging on your outside. Jolt him with the outside shoulder being ready to protect to the inside. Hold your position.

#3 Back: (Righ Footed Kicker) Can assume two positions.

Both 1½ yards behind #2 back. Directly behind or split outside leg of #2 back.

1. Directly behind—Take three steps to the outside, starting with your inside foot and finishing with your inside foot.

2. Splitting outside foot of #2 Back, take two steps starting with your outside foot.

3. Both times finish up with the inside step. Extend wall of blocks set up by line and #2 back. You have the same blocking rule as #1 and #2 backs.

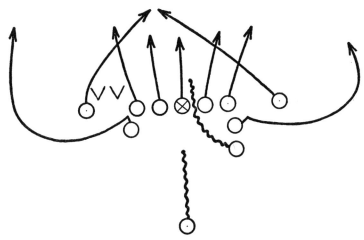

COVERAGE ASSIGNMENTS. ILLUSTRATION #4.

Ends: Cover the kick. Tackle the ball carrier from an outside-in position. Never miss the tackle to the outside. The ball carrier must run inside if you miss the tackle.

Center, Guards and Tackles: Go downfield on the kick of the ball. Spread out to cover the field.

#1 and #2 Backs: Go to your outside on the kick of the ball. Keep outside leverage on the ball carrier.

#3 Back: Do not go downfield too quickly. Stay in front of the ball carrier. You are the first safety man or linebacker.

Kicker: Last safety man. You must stop the ball carrier if the team fails to stop him.

Quick Kick-Blocking Assignments

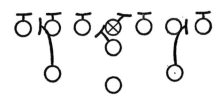

ILLUSTRATION #5.

1. Both sides block like the onside on an inside running play.

2. *Center:* Pass ball through quarterback's legs, protect to your right.

3. *Quarterback:* Protect to your left.

4. *Halfbacks:* Drive straight forward blocking the first man outside of your tackle.

Quick Kick Coverage

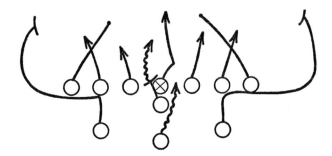

ILLUSTRATION #6.

Assignments same as for the Tight Punt.

1. Quarterback first safety man or linebacker.

2. Kicker second safety man.

Point After Touchdown—Field Goals

ILLUSTRATION #7.

Block assignments same as for tight punt.

Field Goal Coverage

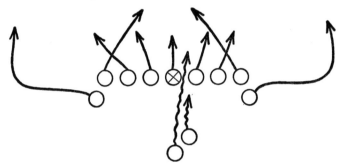

ILLUSTRATION #8.

Coverage same as Tight Punt.

1. Kicker first safety man or linebacker.
2. Ball holder—Second safety man.

Kicking is an offensive phase of football. Many people mistakenly believe that when a team kicks, they are in a sense, surrendering to their opponents. Actually, kicking is an offensive weapon.

When a team kicks off over the goal line, their opponent is 80 yards from the goal line when they put the ball in play. They must move 50 yards to reach the "4 down area." If a team makes a poor kick or allows a long run, their opponent may get the ball at midfield and they are only 20 yards away from the "4 down area."

When a team is deep in their own territory, by quick kicking, they can get the ball over the safety man's head. Again, their opponent will start with a 1st and 10 a long way from their goal.

When a team is not deep in their own territory, but are forced to kick, by good punt protection and coverage, they are insured at least a 35 yard gain from their line of scrimmage. Their opponents will get possession of the ball far behind the 50 yard line.

All kick returns are obviously offensive weapons. By returning kick-offs properly, a team will have the ball within striking distance of the "4 down area". By returning punts effectively, a team can gain vertical field position.

CHAPTER SEVEN

Offensive Line Drills

Basic line drills develop body control, agility and the ability to react with accuracy. These fundamental skills are required for linemen to be able to execute offensive and defensive fundamentals. The following drills are designed to develop the offensive fundamentals for linemen.

1. BOARD DRILLS (The boards are 2 x 12, ten feet long and are beveled along the edges).
    a. *Stance and Starts*—This drill places emphasis on a good stance; on the first step as well as having the offensive linemen maintain the width of his stance as he moves down the board. Linemen must maintain a *good base* when blocking a defensive man.

In setting up this drill, the boards are placed about two and one-half yards apart in a straight row approximately one yard from a white line (line boards to two 5 yards square—*Illustration #1*). The number of boards used will depend on the number of players participating in the drill. Usually, one board for every two or three men. The two or three men will line up one behind the other; the first man being approximately two steps behind the white line.

The coach places himself in a position behind the players so that he will be able to see all of the players doing the drill.

On the command of "Ready", the first man in each row assumes a position ready to approach the line of scrimmage after breaking the huddle. On the command of "Break", they move forward two

53

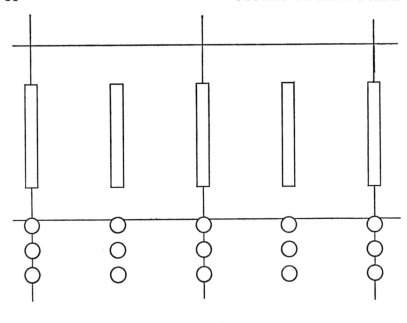

●. *COACH*

ILLUSTRATION #1.

steps placing their feet approximately six inches behind the white line as they assume their offensive stance. On the command of "Hike" (the starting count), they move out of their stance and run over the boards, maintaining the height of their stance as well as keeping their feet as wide as their stance.

The first step would normally be taken with the rear foot and would be twelve to eighteen inches. A lineman must be able to step with either foot first. He must form the habit of taking a six inch step with the proper foot whenever there is a cross charge situation in his area. Since it is unnatural to step with the front foot and to take only a six inch step with either foot, these two fundamentals are stressed first. On the command of "Hike", the players must hit the white line with his first step, stepping with the foot directed by the coach.

The commands are repeated for the next five men during which time, the other men return to their position to repeat the drill. Each player should take eight to ten starts.

2. *One on One Block.* The purpose of this drill is to teach the

fundamentals of the straight one on one shoulder block. The block is executed versus a dummy held by a player. The dummies are placed on the ends of the boards opposite to the end where the players start (*Illustration #2*). The linemen must run down the boards for two yards before making contact. This developes the habit of not stepping for position as well as the habit of not lunging at the defensive man on the one and one block.

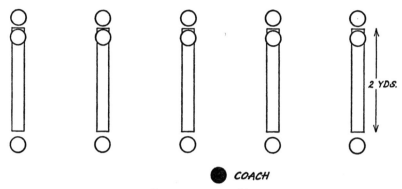

2 YDS.

● COACH

ILLUSTRATION #2.

On the proper commands, the linemen assume their offensive stance at their end of the boards. On the command of "Hike", they move down the boards directing their forehead at a spot, the chin of the defensive man, marked on the dummy. Just before making contact with their forehead, they slide their heads by on the proper slide as directed by the coach. As they make contact with the proper shoulder and arm, using the other arm for balance, they drive the dummy off the end of the board. During which time, they maneuver their feet so that the foot corresponding to the hitting shoulder is in the middle of the dummy (post foot) and the other foot is beyond the dummy (drive foot). Maintaining their foot position, they continue to drive the dummy back for a distance of approximately five yards. They stop on a whistle by the coach.

Each man should execute three or four blocks before changing to the dummy holder. The dummy holder then becomes the blocker. The number of left and right shoulder blocks will depend on the time allotted for the drills. The usual time is ten minutes during which time, each lineman should make ten to twelve straight shoulder blocks. This drill should also be executed by having the offensive linemen assume their stance on the boards at a distance from the dummies that a defensive man would be should he be lined up on the line of scrimmage.

Offensive linemen must learn to execute the one on one straight shoulder block versus defensive linemen who are off-set to one side or the other. Should the defensive man be off-set to one side (outside), the offensive man has a blocking angle should his assignment be to block the defensive man out. The same is true should a defensive man be off-set to the inside, the offensive lineman has a blocking angle should his assignment be to block the defensive man in. In either case, the offensive lineman should step off with his near foot (the foot nearer the defensive man) and *still* direct his forehead for the chin of the defensive man before sliding his head by on the proper side. He should then maneuver his feet into their proper positions.

By doing these fundamentals, the defensive man will not know which way the offensive man is attempting to block him. This should enable the offensive lineman to block in a defensive lineman who is off-set to the outside as well to block out a defensive lineman who is off-set to the inside.

These fundamentals can be taught by the use of the board drill. In setting up these drills, the boards are placed at outside or inside angles to the line of scrimmage depending on the off-set. The offensive linemen assume their stance perpendicular to the line of scrimmage. They are lined up at a normal distance from the dummies which are placed on the end of the boards (*Illustration #3*).

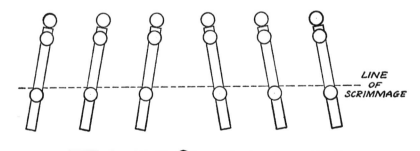

COACH

ILLUSTRATION #3.

The offensive linemen then execute the left and right straight shoulder block by stepping off with the proper foot, directing their forehead for the proper spot before sliding their heads by on the proper side.

Live defensive men can be used in these three board drills. The defensive linemen should assume their stance on the end of the boards where the dummies had been placed. The offensive linemen should line up at a normal distance from the defensive men. When the boards are placed at an angle to the line of scrimmage, both linemen should line up perpendicular to the line of scrimmage. The drills are conducted in the same manner as when the dummies were being used.

3. *Chute Drills.* The chute resembles that of a starting gate for race horses with the exception that it is only 3½ feet high. It is composed of seven individual chutes five feet wide and four feet deep (*Illustration #4*).

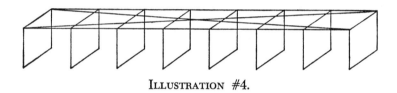

ILLUSTRATION #4.

The chute, referred to as the "monster" by some coaches, is used to teach the offensive linemen the importance of firing straight out from their stance rather than rising up on their initial charge. It also teaches and develops the habit of the offensive linemen to maintain the height of their stance when making contact with the defensive lineman.

The third objective of the chute drill is to develop the entire line to take their proper position on the *line of scrimmage* and to get off together, as a unit, on the starting count.

The drill is set up by placing a board used in the board drill in the middle of each chute so that approximately eighteen inches of the boards extends beyond the rear of the chute. A dummy, which is held by a player, is placed on the board at the rear of the chute. A football is placed in front of the middle board.

As many as three or four lines may participate in the drill. However, it is better to work two lines at one time, one line holding and the other line blocking. This eliminates players standing around and not utilizing valuable practice time (*Illustration #5*).

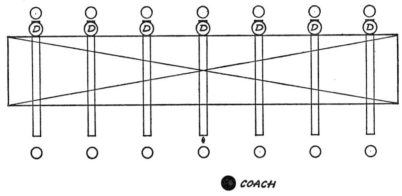

COACH

ILLUSTRATION #5.

The seven linemen doing the blocking place themselves two or three steps behind the ball. The coach puts himself in a position to be able to check the alignment of the offensive line after they have assumed their stance.

On the command of "Ready", the center takes his position over the ball and the other six linemen assume a position ready to approach the line of scrimmage after breaking the huddle. On the command of "Break", the six linemen move forward to the line of scrimmage and assume their stance. On the command of "Hike", the line moves out of their stance, charging through the chutes blocking the dummies with the shoulder directed by the coach. The blockers will stop on a whistle by the coach. Each line should block three or four times before changing with the dummy holders. The total number of blocks will depend on the allotted time for the drill. Each line should have time for at least ten or twelve blocks to accomplish the purpose of the drill.

4. *Live Blocking Drills.* In setting up live offensive line blocking drills, we find it necessary to have ball carriers participate in the drills. This gives the defensive and offensive linemen the incentive to go full speed.

#1 *Live Blocking Drills*—Three hand-off drills, which can be executed at the same time, are set up primarily for offensive line blocking. Each of the three drills have only one offensive lineman blocking a defensive lineman. This gives the coach the opportunity to concentrate on the one offensive lineman so that he can correct his errors and help improve his blocking technique.

Two blocking dummies are required for each drill for defensive spacing. The men required for each group are as follows:

GROUP I —Five or six linemen, a center, quarterback, and two or three left halfbacks. (*Illustration #6*)

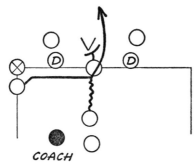

ILLUSTRATION #6.

GROUP II —Same as above (right halfbacks). (*Illustration #7*)

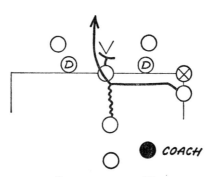

ILLUSTRATION #7.

GROUP III—Three centers, three fullbacks, one quarterback, and three linemen. (*Illustration #8*)

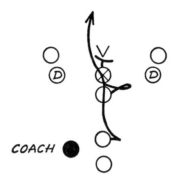

ILLUSTRATION #8.

One lineman is placed in a position behind the defensive lineman so that he can give the play number, when necessary, and the starting count by a hand signal to the offensive linemen. The coach in each group positions himself behind the offensive men so that he will be able to see the offensive linemen.

Each offensive blocker should run three or four plays before rotating with the other linemen. Twelve to fifteen minutes should be allotted for this drill which will enable each lineman to make six or eight offensive blocks.

#2 Live Blocking Drills—These blocking drills are set up as described above with the exception that you now have two offensive blockers versus two defensive men in the halfback drills and three offensive blockers in the fullback drill. In each drill, one of the offensive linemen will now be blocking a linebacker, as directed by the coach, rather than a defensive lineman. (*Illustration #9*).

#3 Live Blocking Drills—The head up, half-line of scrimmage is set up with a complete backfield operating behind one side of the line and center versus the other side of the line and an extra defensive lineman. (*Illustration #10*).

By using a complete backfield, you can run your basic offense, directed by the coach, to the side of the offensive linemen. The usual time allotted for this drill is twelve to fifteen minutes.

Change the linemen halfway through the drill and run the offense to the other side.

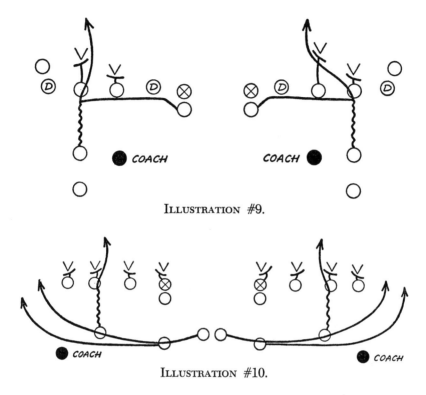

ILLUSTRATION #9.

ILLUSTRATION #10.

The organization of the drill will depend on how strenuous you want to make the drill. Eventually, the drill will be set up so that the left side of the first line will be working against the right side of the first line. However, the first two or three times the drill is used in practice, it can be organized as follows:

GROUP I —Backfield, center and right side of Team #1 vs. Left side of Line #3 and an extra lineman.

GROUP II —Backfield, center of Team #2 and Left side of Line #1 vs. Right side of Line #3 and an extra lineman.

GROUP III—Backfield, center and Right side of Team #3 vs. Left side of Line #4 and an extra lineman.

GROUP IV—Backfield, center of Team #4 and Left side of Line #3 vs. Right side of Line #4 and an extra lineman.

#4 Live Blocking Drill—A complete team versus seven defensive linemen head on the seven offensive linemen.

In this drill, there are seven men excuting the straight one on one shoulder block. The objective of the drill is to have the offensive men block with proper shoulder and to drive their defensive man back maintaining contact until the play is over.

5. Balance Drill—The important factors for having good balance are a good bend at the knees and a wide enough stance to have a good base. On play passes, linemen start their pass protection blocks with the same initial movement as any running play. After contact is made, a lineman must maintain good balance so that he will be able to move to stay directly in front of the defensive man. Any lineman with out-stretched legs is helpless to react until he makes an adjustment after which time, it is too late. The objective of the balance drill is to teach the importance of the fundamentals of good balance and body control.

This drill is set up by having one half of the men participating in the drill to line up in a straight line approximately 2 yards apart. The other men line up opposite them as defensive linemen. (*Illustration #11*).

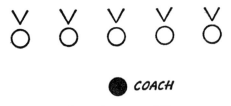

ILLUSTRATION #11.

On the starting count, the offensive men fire out as they would on a play pass making contact with the defensive man. After contact is made, the defensive man attempts to manuever past the offensive man by faking one way and going the other. The offensive man reacts to the defensive man, and if he has good balance, he will be able to stay in front of the defensive man for at least four or five seconds. This is the length of time which is necessary to protect the passer on a play pass. Change the offensive and defensive linemen after three or four times. Each lineman should be on the offensive a total of 10 or 12 times.

6. *Pulling Drills.*

A. *To Trap*—Practice time is most important and every effort must be made to utilize it properly. Therefore, in setting up the trapping drill, we have two men pulling and trapping at the same time.

Since the left guards trap to the right and the right guards trap to the left, the drill is set up with the left guards on the right side of the drill and the right guards on the left side of the drill.

Two blocking dummies are used as defensive men to be trapped. The dummies are held by players and are placed in the different positions that a defensive man may be on a trap play.

Two left guards and two right guards line up at normal distance on the line of scrimmage. The two inside guards are lined up a yard apart and are the pulling men. The two outside guards are playing as centers and have defensive men playing over them when they block.

The coach places himself in a position behind the men so that he can see both men pull and execute their blocks. (*Illustration #12*).

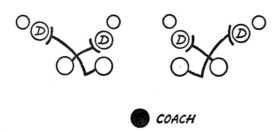

ILLUSTRATION #12.

After each block, the four men participating on either side rotate as follows:

1. Center to the Pulling Guard.
2. The Defensive man to Center
3. The Dummy Holder to the Defensive man.
4. The Trapper to the Dummy Holder.

Each man should make four or five blocks in the alloted time of ten minutes.

B. *To Lead Interference*—Since the courses that pulling line-men take to lead interference will vary on different plays, drills of this type must be organized for particular plays. In setting up the drills, they are organized so that the linemen will pull to the right and left in the same drill.

Six blocking dummies are used to represent defensive men. The dummies are held by players and are placed in the various positions that the defensive men may be on the particular play for which the drill is being done. Two sets of guards line up on the line of scrimmage. The two inside guards line up at their normal spacing and are the first set of guards pulling. After the first set of guards alternate pulling and after making four blocks, two to the right and two to the left, they change with the dummy holders. The total number of blocks will be determined by the time allotted for the drill and the particular play (*Illustration #13*).

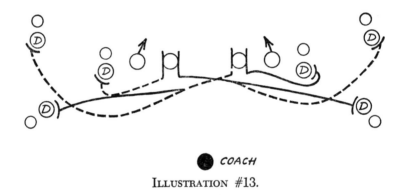

COACH

ILLUSTRATION #13.

7. *Pass Protection and Coverage Drill*—The three important factors that linemen must know on any pass play are:

1. Blocking assignments versus various defenses.

2. The area from which the ball will be passed.

3. The area to which the ball will be passed.

Linemen must be able to recognize the various defensive sets in their area so that they will block the proper defensive man and not allow an unblocked defensive lineman to rush the passer. It is most important that linemen know the area from which the ball will be thrown so that they can block intelligently. The linemen must also know the area to which the ball will be passed so that they can cover the pass properly. This drill accomplishes these three factors placing emphasis on the interior linemen covering the pass in case of an interception after the ball has been thrown. The drill is executed when the backs and ends are running their pass patterns. Two interior lines and two additional linemen used as pass interceptors participate in the drill. (*Illustration #14*)

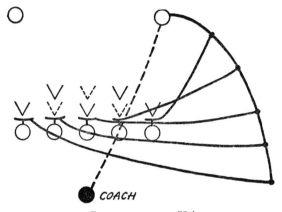

ILLUSTRATION #14.

The coach calls the pass play in the huddle with the offensive line which gives the defensive linemen an opportunity to change their defensive alignments. After the ball has been put in play and the linemen have blocked for the pass called, the coach throws the interception. The offensive linemen then cover the pass. Each lineman must pursue on the proper angle to put himself in position to tackle the interception, to prevent the long return or touchdown. The two lines change after four or five plays.

8. *Cross-Charge Blocking Drill*—To block cross-charging defensive linemen, the two offensive linemen working together must have the proper distance (referred to as cross-charge distance), between them and must move out of their stance with a six inch step with their near foot. These fundamentals are stressed in the cross-charge blocking drill which must be executed at full speed.

This drill is set up with the understanding that both sides of the offensive line is the on-side (the side to which the play will be directed) and the entire line will block the cross-charges with this in mind.

Two complete lines and one additional defensive lineman participate in the drill. The coach positions himself behind the offensive line so that he can see the entire offensive line blocking the cross-charges.

The first part of the drill is organized with the following offensive linemen working against cross-charges in their area:

1. The right end and tackle.
2. The right guard and center.
3. The left guard and tackle.
4. The left end.

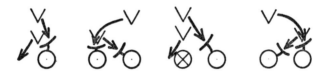

● *COACH*

ILLUSTRATION #15.

The defensive linemen will line up in various cross-charges alignments in the area in which they are working. This is done when offensive linemen are in the huddle getting the starting count from the coach. After blocking four or five cross-charges from this set-up, the offensive linemen change so that the following offensive men are working against cross-charges in their area:

1. The left end and tackle.
2. The left guard and center.
3. The right guard and tackle.
4. The right end.

COACH

ILLUSTRATION #16.

After completing this part of the drill, the two lines change and the drill is repeated. Each line will be able to block eight to ten cross-charges in the allotted time of twelve minutes.

9. *Recognition Drill*—For any offensive play in football to be successful, the offensive line must know their blocking assignments versus the various defenses. In addition to this, a Split "T" lineman must be able to recognize the defensive set in his area so that he can split properly for the defense and the play called.

The purpose of the recognition drill is to give the offensive linemen practice in splitting and to review their blocking assignments versus various defensive alignments. Two complete lines and one additional defensive man participate in the drill. The defensive lineman uses a different defensive alignment each time the offensive line huddles. The offensive line huddles and is given a play number and starting count by the coach.

On the command of "Ready", the offensive linemen turn out of the huddle and look at the defensive alignment in their area. On the command of "Break", they approach the line of scrimmage, take their splits and assume their stance. On the starting count, they block their defensive man for the play called in the huddle. After the play is over, the offensive linemen return to the line of scrimmage, take their splits for the defensive alignment, and assume a kneeling position. The coach then calls different play numbers and the offensive linemen point out their blocking assignments for that particular defense. (*Illustration #17*).

The offensive line huddles again and the drill is repeated against another defensive alignment. The two lines change after the drill has been repeated four or five times versus various defensive alignments.

ILLUSTRATION #17.

10. *Downfield Blocking Drills*—The most important fundamental in downfield blocking is the *course* which the downfield
blocker takes. This course should be a shallow course which will
put the blocker between the ball carrier and the secondary defensive men at the earliest possible moment.

In the downfield blocking drill, the shallow course is emphasized as well as the proper execution of the cross body blocks. In
setting up this drill, the lines are divided into two groups so that
two downfield blocking drills can be done at the same time. The
left side of all lines and half of the centers in another group, and
the right side of all the lines and the other centers in one other
group. The men of three lines line up in the offensive positions
one behind the other. The men of another line line up on
defense.

Two dummies are used in each drill, four of which are held by
linemen and represents defensive secondary men. The first
dummy is placed ten to fifteen yards from the first offensive
blocker and five yards from the line of scrimmage. The other three
dummies are spaced three yards apart on a slight angle from the
line of scrimmage. The fifth dummy is placed horizontally on the
ground five yards from the first offensive man and three yards
from the line of scrimmage. The coaches place themselves in a
position on the line of scrimmage halfway between the offensive
linemen and the dummies downfield so that they can observe their
entire drill (*Illustration #18*).

On the starting count given by the coach, the first group of offensive linemen block through the defensive linemen who attempt
to delay them. They then run their course between the line of
scrimmage and the horizontal dummy and execute a cross body
block on their respective dummies. As the men execute their

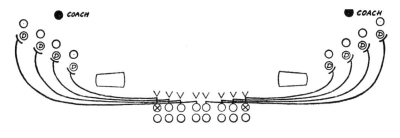

ILLUSTRATION #18.

blocks, the dummy holders will pull the dummies back approx-imately a foot to give the blockers the reaction of live men.

After the blocks have been made, the men rotate as follows:

1. Next offensive group to blockers.
2. Blockers to dummy holders.
3. Dummy holders to defense.
4. Defense to the rear of the offensive groups.

Each linemen should make at least four downfield blocks during the drill.

CHAPTER EIGHT

Signal System, Theory of Splits, Split Rules for Split "T" Formation

There are a great many signal systems used successfully in modern football. The reason for any signal system is to have a simple method of calling the offensive plays and to teach the offensive assignments.

A number of years ago when you could expect to meet a six man line every game, numbering the defensive holes was relatively simple. When teams began to use the four, five and seven man lines, numbering the defense holes became very confusing. In present day football, the various defensive alignments used with the four, five, six, seven and eight man lines are even more perplexing.

There are still teams using the method of numbering the defensive hole with successful results. However, since we have no control over the defense and our offensive linemen will line up relatively in the same position, we number our holes in relation to the outside hip of our offensive linemen. (*Illustration #1*).

In (*Illustration #1*) you will find all even numbered holes are to the right and all odd numbered holes are to the left. The holes are indicated with the high numbers wide and as the number decreases in size, the closer to the middle of the line the play will be directed.

ILLUSTRATION #1.

Our plays are called by a two digit number. The first number indicates the series or type of play and the second digit indicates the hole through which the play will be directed.

To further simplify our signal system, we do not number our backfield men. We feel sure no back will forget when he is to carry the ball. This method enables us to have several series or special plays by changing the first digit of the two digit play number. However, the second digit in the play number will always indicate the hole through which the play will be directed.

All split "T" plays are numbered in the twenty series. The word "pass" is simply added to any play number if we want to fake the running play and throw a pass.

Theory of Offensive Line Splits

The theory of using offensive line splits has one objective. The splits are taken for the purpose of spreading the defense. The two reasons for spreading the defense are: (1) to create holes in the defense before the ball has been snapped and (2) to isolate the defensive man at the critical point of attack.

Splits are not taken to get blocking angles. However, if the defense does not spread with the splits of the offensive line, blocking angles will result. If the offensive line splits to get blocking angles, the two reasons for spreading the defense are lost. Linemen must keep this theory in mind: (1) you split to spread the defense and (2) if the defense does not spread, blocking angles will result.

Most "T" formation have their linemen split. The guards split 1 foot, the tackles 2 feet and the ends 2½–3 feet. These splits are standard and the linemen do not vary them. They do spread the defense to a certain degree, however, we do not consider this a split "T" offensive line.

To further clarify this point and the two reasons for spreading the defense, let's take two examples: (1) The splits versus the two defensive guards on a normal six man line (*Illustration #2A-B*).

ILLUSTRATION 2A-B.

(2) The splits versus the three middle men on the defense referred to as the "Pro" or "Eagle" defense (*Illustration #3A-B*).

ILLUSTRATION 3A-B.

Illustration #3A-B shows the spacing of the two defensive guards when the two offensive guards take a standard split of 1 foot from the center. *Illustrtaion #2B* shows the spacing that results when the two offensive guards split to spread the defense. It is obvious that the space between the two defensive guards is greater when the guards split to spread the defense than when the offensive guards take a standard split of 1 foot.

When an improper split occurs, splitting to get a blocking angle, the offensive guards would move in next to the center to have an inside blocking angle to block the two defensive guards out. When this happens, the two defensive guards would move in with the offensive guards and continue to play head on to them. When this happens, the two offensive guards have accomplished nothing more than to narrow the space between the two defensive guards where the play has been directed (*Illustration #4*).

ILLUSTRATION #4.

Should the defensive guards not choose to split out with the offensive guards, outside blocking angles are inevitable (*Illustration #5*).

ILLUSTRATION #5.

If the play is directed to either side, outside the defensive guards, either offensive guard would have an easy outside blocking angle. The center would also have a blocking angle on the off defense guard. The off defense guard could pull around or go straight downfield to become a downfield blocker (*Illustration #6*).

ILLUSTRATION #6.

When linemen split with the intention to spread the defense and the defensive linemen do not split with them, an outside blocking angle will result.

The second reason for splitting is to isolate the defense man at the critical point of attack. *Illustration #3A* shows the spacing of the three middle men on defense when the two offensive guards take a standard split of 1 foot. *Illustration #3B* shows the spacing when the two offensive guards split to spread the defense. It is apparent that the middle defensive player is isolated when the offensive guards split to spread the defense.

When the play is directed in this area, the two offensive guards contain their defensive men to keep the hole open to either side of the center. The center need do no more than turn the middle defensive man to either side and the ball carrier breaks to the side opposite of the defensive man.

From a defensive standpoint, one of two methods must be used in establishing defensive spacing. A defense man may be instructed to line up on an offensive lineman or to play spacing.

When lining up on an offensive player, he may line up head on, nose on inside shoulder, or nose on inside or outside ear. When playing spacing, he must keep a certain distance between himself and his teammates on either side. Regardless of the splits in the offensive line, he will maintain this distance which may be arm's length, two yards, three yards, or whatever may have been estalished as the most satisfactory distance.

Offensive linemen must determine as soon as possible which of the two methods the defense has been instructed to play. If the defense is using Method One (lining up on the offensive man), it is apparent that the offensive man can maneuver the defensive man to a position which would be advantageous for the play called as the defensive man is concerned only with lining up opposite the offensive man.

If Method Two (play spacing) is being utilized by the defense, maintaining a certain distance between themselves regardless of the splits taken by the offensive line, blocking angles can be obtained by the offensive linemen by varying their splits.

Regardless how the defense has been instructed to play, the offensive linemen should be able to take advantage of the defense if they study the defensive men in their area and will split properly.

Offensive linemen must remember they split to spread the defense. This will create large openings in the defensive line and it is not necessary to block the hole open. The offensive linemen need only to occupy or contain the defensive man since the hole already exists by splitting properly.

Split Rules for Split "T" Formation

Offensive linemen should remember they have the initiative and the advantage of knowing where the play is being directed. By varying their splits on every play, they can maneuver laterally (the defensive men playing opposite them) to a position which is most advantageous for the play called.

The theory of splitting must always be uppermost in their mind. Split to spread the defense, if the defense does not spread, blocking angles will result.

Fundamentally, as far as the five interior offensive linemen are concerned, there are only two basic defensive alignments. These are:

1. An even alignment or two defensive linemen playing head

on the offensive guards. There may or may not be a defensive lineman head on the center (*Illustration #7*).

ILLUSTRATION #7.

2. An odd alignment or a defensive lineman playing head on the center and no defensive lineman on the guards (*Illustration #8*).

ILLUSTRATION #8.

The ends need not be concerned with the interior defensive alignment since the alignment in their area may be the same on an even or odd interior alignment (*Illustration #9*).

ILLUSTRATION #9.

The same is true of the center and guards; they need not be concerned with the alignment in the area of the ends and the center need not be concerned with the alignment of the defense in the area of the tackles.

This being the case, the offensive linemen do not need to know the entire defensive alignment. They need only to be concerned with the defensive alignment in their area. This eliminates the necessity for the quarterback to call the entire defensive alignment for the offensive line or the offensive tackle to call the defensive alignment for his side of the offensive line.

By having each offensive lineman recognize and split for the defensive alignment in his own area, each player can be held responsible for his split as well as his blocking assignment.

Offensive linemen must be able to recognize the three classifications of defensive men. The three catgories are: (1) defensive linemen, (2) linebackers and (3) secondary men. A defensive lineman is any defensive man within 1½ yards of the line of scrimmage. A linebacker is any defensive man whose alignment is between 1½ yards and 4 yards of the line of scrimmage.

Whenever there is a defensive man in the twilight zone of 1½ yards, his defensive stance will determine his classification. Should the player have his hand or both hands on the ground, he would be a lineman. If the opponent is in an erect stance, he would be a linebacker.

Any man deeper than 4 yards would be referred to as a secondary defensive man. Whenever there is any doubt, the defensive man should be played as a linebacker.

Split rules for all offensive linemen are:

1. Never allow any opponent to shoot the gap to your inside.
2. Always try to get an outside angle on your opponent.
3. Always take your maximum split.
4. Stop splitting when you have your maximum angle on your opponent. A lineman will never be able to take his maximum split unless he is unable to get his maximum angle.
5. Cross-Charge distance is 1½ feet from the lineman with whom you are working.

A. The guards split rules are:
   1. Whenever there is a lineman playing on you, split to get a 1/3 of a man angle on him. Your maximum split is four feet.
   2. Whenever there is a linebacker playing opposite you, split to get a full man angle on him. Your maximum side is seven feet.
   3. Whenever there is a cross charge situation in the area of center and you, split cross-charge distance from the center.

B. The tackle split rules are:
   1. Whenever there is a lineman playing on you, split to get a man angle on him. Your maximum split is 4 feet.

    2. Whenever there is a linebacker playing opposite you, split to get a full man angle on him. Your maximum split is 6 feet.

    3. Whenever there is a cross-charge situation in the area of your guard and you, split cross-charge distance from the guard.

C. The ends split rules are:

    1. Whenever there is a lineman on you, split to get a 2/3 angle on him. Your maximum split is 4 feet.

    2. Whenever there is a linebacker playing opposite you, split to get a 1/2 man angle on him. Your maximum split is three feet.

    3. Whenever there is a cross-charge situation in the area of your tackle and you, split cross-charge distance from your tackle.

In most offenses, a lineman is instructed to where and how to line up and is not given the freedom of movement along the line of scrimmage. There are times when the defensive man against whom he is playing may be physically stronger and will defeat him regardless of how hard he may try.

Split "T" linemen, if they are intelligent enough to split properly, should never feel that they can be dominated by a physically superior opponent.

A Split "T" lineman, by experimenting with his splits when he is on the off-side can learn the reactions of a defensive man to the various positions he takes. By gaining and using this knowledge, he can place the defensive man at a disadvantage and will be able to block or occupy him when the play is directed to his side.

Most linemen would rather play on defense than offense. Linemen who have the opportunity to play on the Split "T" offense enjoy playing offense. They feel by having freedom of lateral movement along the line of scrimmage, they can out-maneuver and out-smart defensive line men.

CHAPTER NINE

Recognition of Defensive Sets

There are a variety of methods to teach blocking assignments used in present day football. Each has its own advantage. The purpose of any method is to simplify blocking rules to eliminate offensive assignment errors.

Blocking assignments for the basic defenses are not difficult. It is the variations of alignments used from the basic defenses which are confusing and cause offensive linemen to miss blocking assignments.

The offensive line need not be concerned with the entire alignment of the defense. They need be concerned only with the defensive alignment in their area. The guards and centers, the tackles and guards, and the ends and tackles must work together.

On a normal even defense, the defensive alignment in the area of the guards and center would have two defensive linemen lined up head on the offensive guards. The end and tackle may have several different alignments in their area. The defense could be a wide tackle six, having the defensive tackle head on the end and the linebacker head on the tackle. The defense could be a tight tackle six, having the tackle head on the tackle and the linebacker head on the end. In either of these alignments, the linebacker may line up on the line. Another alignment could find the defensive tackle lined up between the tackle and the end with the linebacker lined up directly behind the defensive tackle making it a cross-charge situation.

From an over all defensive alignment, if the linebacker lines up off the line of scrimmage, the defense would be called a 6-2-2-1. If the linebackers line up on the line of scrimmage, it would be called an 8-3 defense. In either defense, the guards and center have the same blocking assignments and the guards have the same split rule. The ends' and tackles' assignments for blocking and splits would vary with each defensive alignment in their area even though the basic defense is a 6-2-2-1.

In order to further clarify this point, let's take another example of a situation where there are two defensive linemen lined up head on the offensive tackle and end. When this defensive set is used in the area of the tackle and end, there are several defensive alignments which can be used in the area of the guards and center.

The defense could be an odd alignment with a lineman head on the center and two linebackers lined up head on the guards or an even alignment with two linemen head on the guards and a linebacker lined up head on the center. These three defensive men can change their alignments in several ways which will be discussed in the defensive sets. Regardless of the different alignments in the area of the guards and center, the blocking assignments and split rule remain the same for the tackle and ends. The guards and center will now have to change their blocking assignments versus the various alignments in their area. The guards will also have to adjust their splits.

These examples illustrate that it is unnecessary for the offensive line to know the entire defense since their blocking assignments are in no way affected by the defensive alignments or sets not in their area.

The various defensive alignments with which offensive linemen may be confronted must be recognized quickly to determine their split and blocking assignment. There is little time after they break the huddle before the ball is snapped.

The purpose of defensive sets is to simplify the recognition of defensive alignments and blocking assignments. The sets used should cover any possible defensive alignment that offensive linemen may see in their area.

The various defensive alignments with which offensive linemen may be confronted must be recognized quickly to determine their split and blocking assignment. There is little time after they break the huddle before the ball is snapped.

The purpose of defensive sets is to simplify the recognition of defensive alignments and blocking assignments. The sets used should cover any possible defensive alignment that offensive line-men may see in their area.

Defensive Sets for the Center

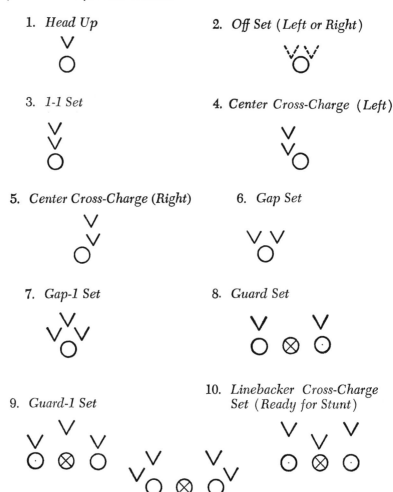

1. *Head Up*

2. *Off Set (Left or Right)*

3. *1-1 Set*

4. *Center Cross-Charge (Left)*

5. *Center Cross-Charge (Right)*

6. *Gap Set*

7. *Gap-1 Set*

8. *Guard Set*

9. *Guard-1 Set*

10. *Linebacker Cross-Charge Set (Ready for Stunt)*

11. *Wide Guard Set*

Defensive Sets for Guards

1. *1-1 Set*

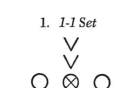

2. *Gap Set*

3. *Gap-1 Set*

4. *Center Cross-Charge*

5. *Guard Set (May or may not be man on Center)*

6. *Guard-1 Set*

7. *Even Cross-Charge*

8. *Backer Cross-Charge*

9. *Guard Cross-Charge*

10. *Wide Guard*

11. *Outside Gap*

Defensive Sets for Tackles

1. *Even Cross-Charge*

2. *Wide Guard*

3. *Double Gap*

4. *Guard Cross-Charge*

5. *Head Up Set*

6. *3-1 Set*

7. *Linebacker Cross-Charge Set*

8. *Covered Cross-Charge*

9. *Linebacker Set*

10. *Tackle Cross-Charge Set*

Defensive Sets for Ends

1. *Gap Set*

2. *Tackle Cross-Charge*

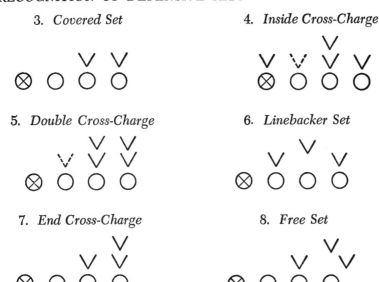

3. *Covered Set*

4. *Inside Cross-Charge*

5. *Double Cross-Charge*

6. *Linebacker Set*

7. *End Cross-Charge*

8. *Free Set*

These sets cover the basic defenses and the possible alignments from these defenses which may be used in the area of each offensive man. Since the guards and center, the tackles and guards, and the ends and tackles must work together, the same sets, in some instances, must be used.

CENTER SETS:

1. *Head Up*—The "Pro" or "Eagle" Defense.
2. *Off-Set*—The 6-2 Defense with a half-a-man overshift.
3. *One-One Set*—The 5-3; 7-1; and the 6-2 Defense with a full man overshift.
4. *Center Cross-Charge (Left or Right)*—The variations used from the 6-1 and Oklahoma 5-4 Defense.
5. *Gap Set*—the 8-3 Goal Line Defense.
6. *Gap One Set*—The variation used from a 6-1 Defense
7. *Guard Set*—The 6-2 and 8-3 Defense.
8. *Guard One Set*—The 6-1 Defense.
9. *Linebacker Cross-Charge Set*—Oklahoma 5-4 Defense.
10. *Wide Guard Set*—The variation used from the 6-2 Defense.

GUARD'S SETS WHICH ARE NOT COVERED UNDER CENTER SETS:

1. *Even Cross-Charge*—The 4-4 Defense on a variation used from the 6-2 Defense.
2. *Guard Cross-Charge*—The variation used from the Oklahoma 5-4 Defense.
3. *Outside Gap*—"Pro" or "Eagle" Defense.

TACKLE SETS WHICH ARE NOT COVERED UNDER CENTER AND GUARD SETS:

1. *Double Gap*—"Pro" or "Eagle" and 8-3 Goal Line Defenses.
2. *Head Up Set*—The 6-1 or 8-3 Defense.
3. *Three-One Set*—5-3; 7 Diamond; and the 6-2 Defense with a full man overshift.
4. *Linebacker Cross-Charge Set*—Oklahoma 5-4 Defense.
5. *Covered Cross-Charge*—The variation used from Oklahoma 5-4 and 6-2 Defenses.
6. *Linebacker Set*—The 6-2 Defense (wide tackle).
7. *Tackle Cross-Charge*—Variation used from 6-2 Defense.

END SETS NOT COVERED UNDER THE TACKLE SETS:

1. *Gap Set*—"Pro" or "Eagle" and 8-3 Goal Line Defenses.
2. *Covered Set*—The Oklahoma 5-4, 8-3, 7-1 Defenses.
3. *Inside Cross-Charge*—The Variations used from Oklahoma 5-4 and 6-2 Defenses.
4. *Double Cross-Charge*—The variation used from the Oklahoma 5-4 Defense.
5. *End Cross-Charge*—The variation used from the 5-3 Defense.
6. *Free Set*—The 5-3 Defense.

CHAPTER TEN

Blocking Rules and Assignments

The general blocking rules for the offensive linemen are:

1. Block man over you or the man in your inside gap.
2. If no man over you or in the gap to your inside, go down-field.
3. "A Blocking" center and guard, change blocking assignments.
4. "B Blocking" guard and tackle, change blocking assignments.
5. "C Blocking" tackle and end, change blocking assignments.

The blocking assignments for the center versus the various sets are:

1. *Head up*—Block defensive man away from play.

2. *Off-Set Left or Right*—Blocking angle; block defensive man in gap away from play. No blocking angle; go downfield.

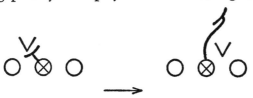

3. *One-One Set*—Block man over you away from play. Cross-Charge; block man cross-charging away from play.

4. *Center Cross-Charge Left or Right*—Block lineman in gap toward play. Block linebacker away from play.

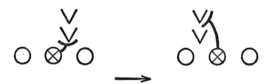

5. *Gap Set*—Block man in gap away from play.

6. *Gap One Set*—Block man in gap towards play.

7. *Guard Set*—Block defensive lineman away from play. "A" Blocking may be used.

8. *Guard One Set*—Block defensive lineman away from play. "A" Blocking may be used.

9. *Linebacker Cross-Charge Set*—Block man over you away from play. Cross-Charge; block man cross-charging towards play.

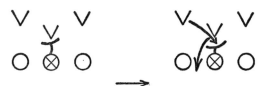

10. *Wide Guard*—Block linebacker away from play.

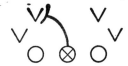

Blocking assignments for the guards versus the various sets are:

On Guard

1. *One-One Set*—Block linebacker. Cross-Charge; block man cross-charging towards play.

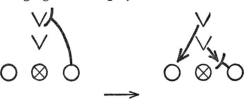

2. *Gap Set*—Block man in gap.

3. *Gap One Set*—Block linebacker.

4. *Center Cross-Charge*—Block linebacker.

5. *Guard Set*—Block man over you away from play.

6. *Guard One Set*—Block man over you away from play.

7. *Even Cross-Charge*—Block man over you. Cross-Charge; block man cross-charging to the inside.

8. *Backer Cross-Charge*—Block linebacker. Cross-Charge; block man cross-charging inside.

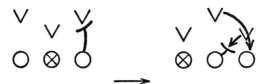

9. *Guard Cross-Charge*—Block man in gap. Cross-Charge; block man cross-charging inside.

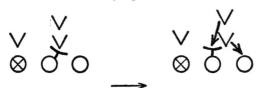

10. *Wide Guard*—Double team with the tackle the man in the gap.

11. *Outside Gap*—Block man in the gap to your outside.

Off-Side Guard

1. *One-One Set*—Block first man outside.

2. *Gap Set*—Block man in gap away from play. If no man in gap, go downfield.

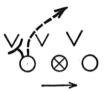

3. *Gap One Set*—Block man in gap.

4. *Center Cross-Charge*—Block man in gap.

5. *Guard Set*—Pull around center, go downfield. "A" blocking may be used.

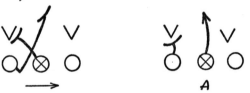

6. *Guard One Set*—Pull around center, block linebacker. "A" blocking may be used.

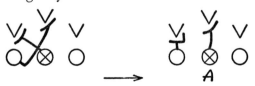

7. *Even Cross-Charge*—Block man over you away from play. Cross-Charge; block man cross-charging towards play.

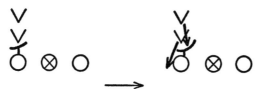

8. *Backer Cross-Charge*—Block first man to your outside. "B" Blocking may be used.

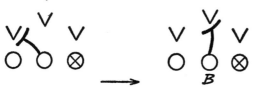

9. *Guard Cross-Charge*—Block man in gap. Cross-Charge; block man cross-charging toward play.

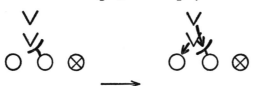

10. *Wide Guard*—Block man in gap.

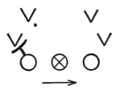

11. *Outside Gap*—Block man in gap.

The blocking assignments for the tackles versus the various sets are:

On-Side Tackle.

1. *Even Cross-Charge*—Block linebacker. Cross-Charge; block man cross-charging towards play.

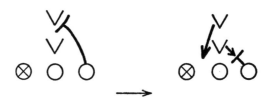

2. *Wide Guard*—Double team with guard the man in the gap.

3. *Double Gap*—Block man in the gap to your outside.

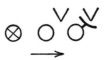

4. *Guard Cross-Charge*—Block linebacker. Cross-Charge; block man cross-charging toward play.

5. *Head Up Set*—Block man over you.

6. *Three-One Set*—Block man over you.

7. *Linebacker Cross-Charge Set*—Block man over you. Cross-Charge; block linebacker.

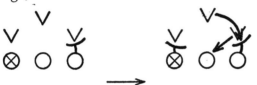

8. *Covered Cross-Charge*—Block man over you. Cross-Charge; block man cross-charging outside. Man over guard, block man cross-charging inside.

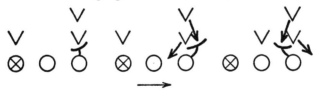

9. *Linebacker Set*—Block linebacker. Cross-Charge; block man cross-charging inside.

10. *Tackle Cross-Charge Set*—Block man in gap. Cross-Charge; block man cross-charging inside.

Off-Side Tackle.

1. *Even Cross-Charge*—Go downfield.

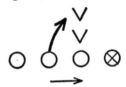

2. *Wide Guard*—Go downfield.

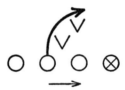

3. *Double Gap*—Block man in the gap to your outside.

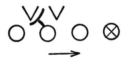

4. *Guard Cross-Charge*—Go downfield.

5. *Head-Up Set*—Block man over you.

6. *Three-One Set*—Pull around guard. Go downfield.

7. *Linebacker Cross-Charge Set*—Pull around guard. Go downfield. "B" blocking may be used.

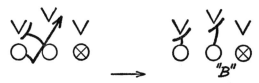

8. *Covered Cross-Charge Set*—Block man over you. Cross-Charge; go downfield.

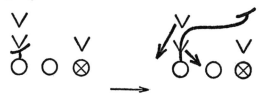

9. *Linebacker Set*—Go downfield.

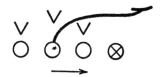

10. *Tackle Cross-Charge*—Block linebacker. Cross-Charge; go downfield.

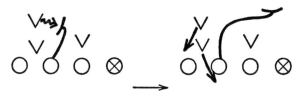

The blocking assignments for the ends versus the various sets are:

On-Side End

1. *Gap Set*—Block man to your outside. Goal Line Defense 8-3; block man in the gap to your inside.

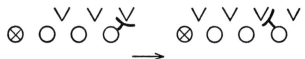

2. *Tackle Cross-Charge*—Block linebacker. Cross-Charge; outside plays—block man cross-charging outside—inside plays —go downfield.

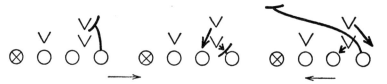

3. *Covered Set*—Block man over you away from play.

4. *Inside Cross-Charges*—Block man over you away from the play. Man over guard; cross-charge. Block the man over the tackle cross-charging outside.

5. *Double Cross-Charge Set*—Block man over you away from the play. Cross-Charge; block man cross-charging inside. Man over guard; cross-charge. Block the man over the tackle cross-charging outside.

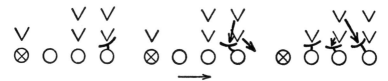

6. *Linebacker Set*—Block man over you away from the play. Cross-Charge; outside play—block linebacker—inside play —go downfield.

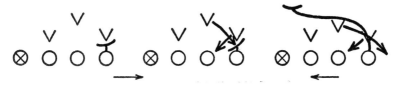

7. *End Cross-Charge*—Block man over you away from play. Cross-Charge; block man cross-charging inside.

8. *Free Set*—Block linebacked away from the play.

Off-Side End—Versus all sets, block through any defensive man in your area before releasing downfield on a shallow course that will get you in front of the ball carrier as quickly as possible.

CHAPTER ELEVEN

Defensive Nomenclature

Defensive terms which describes defensive play.

1. *Head Up*—A position taken by a defensive lineman when he lines up exactly opposite his opponent.
2. *Off the Line*—A position taken by a defensive lineman when he is one foot or more off the line of scrimmage.
3. *Shade Inside (Outside)*—Position taken by a defensive lineman when he lines up with his feet just inside (outside) the feet of the offensive lineman.
4. *On Inside Shoulder (Outside)*—Position taken by a defensive lineman when he lines up with the inside (outside) foot of the offensive lineman in the middle of his stance.
5. *Control Man*—A charge taken by a defensive man which enables him to protect either side of the offensive man.
6. *Control One Side*—A charge taken by a defensive man which enables him to avoid being blocked in one direction.
7. *Slant (Right or Left)*—An angle charge by a defensive lineman into the head of the lineman to either side of his offensive opponent.
8. *Loop (Left or Right)*—A lateral charge taken by a defensive lineman to get past the head of the lineman to either side of his offensive opponent.
9. *Penetrate*—Charge taken by a defensive lineman where he attempts to get into the opponent's backfield rather than controlling his opponent and then pursuing the ball.

10. *"X" Charge (Left or Right)*—A penetrating angle charge by a defensive lineman into the hip of the offensive lineman to either side of his offensive opponent.

11. *"Y" Charge (Left or Right)*—A lateral penetrating charge taken by a defensive man to get past the head of his offensive opponent and into the opponent's backfield.

12. *Flat Charge*—An angle charge taken by a defensive lineman at the juncture of the neck and shoulder of the offensive lineman to either side of his offensive opponent.

13. *Goal Line Charge*—A penetrating dip charge taken by a defensive lineman from a four point stance.

14. *Rush*—Charge taken by a defensive player who makes an all-out attempt to get to the passer before he can throw the ball.

15. *Crash*—A quick forcing charge at a spot one yard behind the quarterback taken by a defensive end when he does not have outside responsibility and can play recklessly.

16. *Tight*—A quick forcing charge at a spot one yard in front of the fullback taken by a defensive end. The end must keep leverage on the fullback.

17. *Spin-Out*—A maneuver used by a defensive lineman to recover when his opponent has outside position and has blocked him out of the play.

18. *Draw Man*—The lineman charged with the responsibility of stopping the draw play.

19. *Flatfooted*—When the defensive end takes one step across the line of scrimmage and then waits for the play to develop before reacting.

20. *Leverage Man*—The player charged with the responsibility of maintaining outside position on the ball.

21. *Corner Man*—The man charged with outside responsibility on a box secondary defense. He is a combination end and halfback.

22. *Force to Sideline*—Course taken by a defensive man who does not have leverage and who is trying to force the ball carrier out of bounds while being sure that he does not cut back into the field.

23. *Angle of Pursuit*—Course taken by defensive linemen which enables them to get to the ball carrier in the shortest possible distance from their original position.

24. *Cut-Off*—Same as Angle of Pursuit. Course taken by a defensive player to catch a ball carrier who does not run in his immediate area.

25. *Osky*—The signal called by a player who is positive he can intercept a forward pass. When other men hear the signal, they should start blocking immediately.

26. *Bingo*—The signal which indicates every defensive player will try to force a fumble by the offense on the next play.

Defensive terms which describe the offensive formations.

1. *Balanced Line*—A set where the center is the middle man of the offensive line. *(Illustration #1)*

1. O O O □ O O O

ILLUSTRATION #1.

2. *Unbalanced Line (Left or Right)*—A set where four (4) offensive men are on one side of the center and two (2) on the other side. *(Illustration #2)*

2. O O O O □ O O

ILLUSTRATION #2.

3. *Five-One Line (Left or Right)*—A set where five (5) offensive linemen are on one side of the center and only one man is on the other side. *(Illustration #3)*

3. O O O O O □ O

ILLUSTRATION #3.

4. *Wingback*—A backfield man who places himself in position to double team block with a lineman.

a. *Normal Wingback*—A back who takes his position a

yard behind the line of scrimmage and three (3) yards or less outside his own end. *(Illustration #4)*

ILLUSTRATION #4.

b. *Inside Wingback*—A back who takes his normal position as a wingback to his tackle when the end is split. *(Illustration #5)*

ILLUSTRATION #5.

5. *Flankered Back*—Whenever a backfield man lines up three (3) yards or more outside his own end.

6. *On Halfback*—Whenever a halfback lines up as a flanker or wingback to his *own* side (On Left—On Right). *(Illustration #6)*

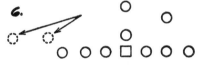

ILLUSTRATION #6.

7. *Crossed Halfback*—Whenever a halfback lines up as a flanker or wing to the opposite side. (Crossed Left-Crossed Right) *(Illustration #7)*

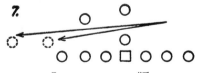

ILLUSTRATION #7.

8. *Fullback Out*—(Left or Right) Whenever the fullback lines up as a flanker or wingback to either side *(Illustration #8)*.

ILLUSTRATION #8.

9. *Split End*—Whenever the end lines up three (3) yards or more from his tackle *(Illustration #9).*

ILLUSTRATION #9.

10. *Slot Back*—Whenever a backfield man lines up three (3) yards or more from the formation inside a split end *(Illustration #10).*

ILLUSTRATION #10.

11. *Flankered Tackle*—Whenever the tackle lines up two (2) yards or more from his guard (*Illustration #11*).

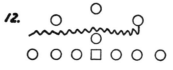

ILLUSTRATION #11.

12. *Flier*—When any man goes in motion before the ball is snapped *(Illustration #12).*

ILLUSTRATION #12.

13. *"T" Formation*—A backfield set up with the quarterback behind the center in a position to take the ball on a hand-back. The line may be balanced, unbalanced or five-one. The ends may be split or the backs set in any variation of flankers *(Illustration #13).*

ILLUSTRATION #13.

14. *Single Wing*—A backfield alignment without a "T" Formation Quarterback. One back is set as a wing back and the inside backs are set in a tandem *(Illustration #14)*.

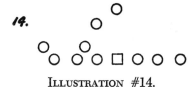

ILLUSTRATION #14.

15. *Box Backfield*—A single wing pattern where the tailback and fullback are the same depth behind the lines of scrimmage and can spin and fake to each other *(Illustration #15)*.

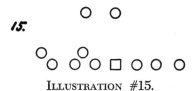

ILLUSTRATION #15.

16. *Double Wing*—A backfield alignment with two backs set as wingbacks. The ends may be normal or split *(Illustration #16)*.

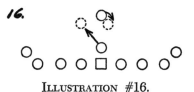

ILLUSTRATION #16.

17. *Spread Formation*
   a. No one under the center and three or more men detached from the formation *(Illustration #17)*.

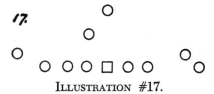

ILLUSTRATION #17.

b. Four men detached from the formation regardless of the quarterback *(Illustration #18)*.

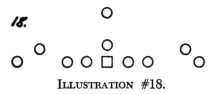

ILLUSTRATION #18.

18. *Short Punt*—A backfield alignment with one man six (6) yards deep, two (2) backs playing parallel to each other three (3) yards deep, and one back directly behind the line to one side or the other of the center *(Illustration #19)*.

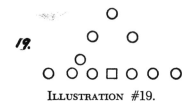

ILLUSTRATION #19.

19. *Deep Punt*—A backfield set up with the deep man ten (10) yards back, the other backs in the same position as described for short punt.

20. *Spread Punt*—A split line between the guards, tackles and ends. Two backs in the gaps between the center and guards. One back six (6) yards deep. (All three backs may be 6 yards deep) *(Illustration #20)*.

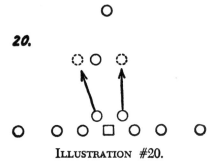

ILLUSTRATION #20.

Defensive Terms which describe Basic Offensive Plays.

1. *Trap*—A play where a defensive line is drawn across the line of scrimmage by a fake and then blocked from the inside or outside by a pulling lineman or a back.

2. *Draw*—A play where a pass is faked. The offensive linemen pass protection block the rushing linemen turning them to the outside. This enables the ball carrier to break between the defensive linemen as they rush.

3. *Screen Pass*—A play where a long downfield pass is faked and the ball is thrown over the heads of the rushing linemen to an eligible receiver on or behind the line of scrimmage.

4. *Eligible Receiver*—Any man eligible to catch a forward pass. This includes the four backfield man with the exception of the "T" Quarterback, and the two men who are in the end's position on the line of scrimmage.

5. *Sideline Cut*—A pass course where the receiver runs quickly down the field until the halfback has to retreat rapidly at which time the receiver makes a sharp break to the outside on a course slightly back toward the line of scrimmage.

6. *Hook*—A pass cut where the receiver rushes downfield until the secondary starts to drop back quickly at which time, the receiver stops quickly, turns back toward the line of scrimmage, and catches the ball.

7. *Flat Pass*—Any pass thrown to a receiver in the area outside of the defensive ends within six (6) yards of the line of scrimmage.

8. *Flare Pass*—A play where the fullback or a halfback loops into the flat as a pass receiver.

9. *Roll-Out Pass*—A play where the quarter swings wide around end with the option to pass or run.

10. *Swing Pass*—A play where the quarterback moves in the same direction as the backfield's first movement and then swings back away from the flow of the backfield with the option to pass or run.

11. *Statue of Liberty*—A play where a pass or kick is faked and the ball is given to a back running wide around the defensive end.

12. *Naked Reverse*—A play where all of the blockers start to one side and the ball is given to a lone ball carrier coming back to the opposite side with little or no interference.

13. *Counter Play*—A play where the quarterback fakes to a halfback driving straight ahead, then turns back and gives the ball to the fullback to the opposite side.

14. *Fullback Cross Buck*—A play where the quarterback fakes to a halfback going across the formation pattern, then gives the ball to the fullback hitting in the opposite direction of the faking halfback.

15. *Halfback Cross Buck*—A play where the quarterback fakes the ball to the fullback hitting in to one side, then gives the ball to the halfback on that side hitting to the opposite side of the fullback's fake.

16. *Inside Belly*—A play where the quarterback may fake or give the ball to the fullback hitting straight in to one side of the quarterback. Should he fake the ball, he then gives it to the far halfback hitting in just outside the fullback. The other halfback is used as a blocker.

17. *Outside Belly*—A play where the quarterback may fake or give the ball to the fullback hitting in off-tackle. Should the quarterback keep the ball, he runs wide around the end to the same side. He also has the option of lateralling the ball to the far halfback who is tracking him. The other halfback is used as a blocker.

18. *Shovel Pass*—A forward pass thrown to a receiver who is normally behind the line of scrimmage.

19. *Quick Kick*—An unexpected punt from a team's regular offensive formation

20. *On-Side Kick*—An attempt by the kicking team to recover their own kick-off after the ball has gone ten (10) yards.

CHAPTER TWELVE

Theory of Defensive Line Play

The foundation of any good football team is defense.

Theoretically, the game of football is divided into three (3) phases. These are (1) defense, (2) offense, and (3) the kicking game. It is my opinion that defense is the most important single phase of the game. It is obvious that if the defense is strong enough, your opponent will not score. If your opponent does not score, your team cannot be defeated. Should your opponents score and your team defense is sound, it is impossible for them to score enough points so that your team cannot maintain an opportunity to win. Before you can use your offense, your team must stop your opponent and gain possession of the ball.

I believe it is agreed that the first objective for all defensive football is to prevent your opponent from scoring. We realize that our opponents will score, but we do not want them to be able to score an easy touchdown with a long pass or run.

The second objective of the defense, which is most important, is to get possession of the ball. This may be done four different ways:

1. Forcing your opponent to kick.
2. Keeping your opponent from making a first down.
3. Recovering a fumble.
4. Intercepting a pass.

The fact that a team is on defense, they have but one thought in their mind and that is to keep the other team from scoring. Gaining possession of the ball is often overlooked by the players, and it is necessary to stress this point with them.

The third objective of the defense is to score. The possibility of scoring when the other team has the ball is also overlooked by the players on defense. Actually, the defense can score in more ways than the offense. The defense can score by (1) intercepting a pass and returning it for a touchdown, (2) returning a kick for a touchdown, (3) blocking a kick and recovering it for a touchdown and (4) forcing a fumble and catching the ball before it hits the ground to score.

There have been many teams whose offense has been stopped, but have won the game with the touchdowns scored by the defense.

Defense is by far the most difficult phase of the game to play successfully.

The offense must and does have two threats through running and passing. The offense knows what type of play they are going to execute. The offense knows where the play will be directed and when the ball will be snapped. Because of these factors, the offense has the initiative. Because the offense does have the initiative, the defense must react to the movement of the offensive team after the ball is snapped. Every defensive alignment must be able to maintain proper balance to defend against a pass and a run at the same time.

Because of the rules of modern football, most coaches will agree that the offense has a distinct advantage over the defense. Since this is the case, most defenses are played with the thought of containing the opponent rather than attempting to throw them for repeated losses. A defense designed to do this will probably succeed three out of four times. However, against such a defense, these few plays which succeed at all will probably go for long gains or touchdowns because the defense has committed itself so strongly along the line of scrimmage. Defensive teams that can prevent the "easy touchdown" are difficult to score against and they are seldom defeated.

Defense is Made up of Two Units

There are a great many variations of defensive alignments used in modern football. The variety can be accounted for through the different types of football ability on the part of the individual players and the fact that different defensive alignments seem to be better against the various offensive formations.

However, regardless of the defensive alignment, a very sound defense is made of two distinct units. These are the containing unit and the forcing unit.

1. CONTAINING UNIT. They are the last line of defense and should have only one pattern of play. With only one pattern of play, they should make fewer errors and should be able to prevent the "easy touchdown" which is vital to the success of any defense.

A containing unit can be composed of four or five defensive men. Regardless of how many men are used, they must coordinate and play together keeping the entire offensive team in front of and inside of them.

On a Box Secondary Defense, the two corner men and two safeties make up the four man containing unit.

On a Three Deep Defense, the two ends and the three deep backs are involved in the five man containing unit.

2. FORCING UNIT. When a four man containing unit is used, seven men remain on to play in the forcing unit. The forcing unit can use several alignments and may play in a variety of ways. The most normal alignments are:

1. A Five Man Line—Two Linebackers.
2. A Six Man Line—One Linebacker.
3. A Four Man Line—Three Linebackers.
4. A Seven Man Line—No Linebackers.

When five men are in the containing unit, only six men are in the forcing unit. Consequently, when played normally, the containing unit will probably contain the offensive team better, but will be unable to force nearly as well. The reverse is true when only four men are used in the containing unit and seven men in the forcing unit. The containing unit will probably not be able to contain the offensive team as well, but the seven men in the forcing unit will be able to more effectively force the issue at the line of scrimmage.

Although the two ends are part of the five man containing unit, their normal alignment is in the line of scrimmage, on or outside the offensive end. From this alignment, they can and are used in the forcing unit leaving only the three deep backs in the containing unit. The normal alignments used by the forcing unit when the five man containing unit is used are:

1. Seven Man Line—One Linebacker.
2. Six Man Line—Two Linebackers.
3. Five Man Line—Three Linebackers.

A great number of variations of alignments can be used from the groups listed above. From these various alignments, many defensive stunts and cross-charges may be used.

When the ends are included in the forcing unit, they are usually used in a defensive stunt. The stunts usually will involve one other defensive man; either the tackle or the linebacker. Occasionally, the stunt may include the entire line and linebackers when an eight man rush is used.

The Forcing Unit Must: (Linemen and Linebackers)

1. PREVENT A SERIES OF FIRST DOWNS. The second objective of the defense is to get possession of the ball. The forcing unit must not allow the offensive team to maintain possession of the ball by making a series of first downs.

They must charge the offensive men hard enough to be able to make the tackle at the line of scrimmage or penetrate quickly enough to get to the ball carrier behind the line of scrimmage. They must not allow the ball carrier to pick up a succession of short gains which will result in a series of first downs.

To accomplish this, the forcing unit must use various alignments and change their angle of their defensive charges. The number of variations used will depend on how many your team can execute and not make mistakes which will cause your team more difficulty than your opponent.

2. CREATE THE "SIX YARD SITUATION." Most good offensive teams will average three or four yards per play which is enough to average a first down every three plays.

The forcing unit of the defense must create a situation where the offense will be required to make six yards or more per try to make a first down. When the offense must average six yards or more per try, the forcing unit has created the "Six Yard Situation."

This situation can be accomplished in two ways; the first of which, the forcing unit has no control. (1) The offensive team is penalized which forces them into a "six yard situation." (2) The second way is by the forcing unit using a penetrating, cross-charge or stunt defense to force an error by offensive teams to enable them to break through and throw the ball carrier for a loss. When your opponent is in the "six yard situation," your defense should play a control defense with the full realization that should the offensive team make only a five yard gain, they have made a successful defensive play.

3. FORCE FUMBLES. Fumbles are forced by the defense when the tackler executes the fundamentals of tackling properly.

The tackler should drive his head through the ball. This will always have him hitting the ball carrier with his shoulder eliminating the so-called arm tackle. He will also be able to drive the ball out of the hands of the ball carrier if he hits sharply enough.

4. RUSH PASSER TO CAUSE THE INTERCEPTION. In rushing the passer, the forcing unit must, after avoiding the offensive blocker, go in high at the passer. This will make it difficult for the passer to see downfield and locate his receivers. It will also make the passer arch the ball higher to get it over the head of the pass rushers. This will give the secondary men, the containing unit, time to move to the ball while it is in the air and make the interception or defend successfully against the pass.

Should the passer throw the ball before the forcing unit can get to him, they should turn and go to where the ball is thrown. By doing this, they may be able to make the tackle which will prevent a touchdown or throw the key block which will enable an interception to go all the way for the touchdown.

5. BLOCK KICKS. The third objective of the defense is to score while on defense. One of the ways this can be done is by blocking a kick and recovering it for a touchdown. This can only be done by the forcing unit.

There are various block kick alignments which may be used to attempt to block kicks. This important factor in attempting to block a kick is to know and to go to the area from which a kick can be blocked. This area is approximately three yards in front of where the kicker lines up and not at the kicker.

Regardless of the alignment being used, each lineman will execute the same fundamentals.

1. GOOD STANCE. Since the offensive blocker is just the length of a football away from the defensive lineman and knows the starting count, it is obvious that the defensive man will be defeated by the offensive blocker if he does not assume a good stance. The offensive blocker will be able to make contact with the defensive man before he can adjust and recover his balance from a bad position.

A good defensive stance is one with proper balance that will enable the defensive man to charge quickly and at the same time, defend himself against his opponent.

2. MOVE WITH THE SNAP OF THE BALL. A defensive lineman must watch carefully the three offensive linemen in his area and at the same time be able to see the ball. As the ball is snapped, the defensive man must start his charge forward. As he makes his first move, which is directed at the opponent directly in front of him, he must see the offensive men on either side of him and key them. The key for any defensive lineman is the movement of the offensive linemen in his area.

Should either offensive man drive at him, he should react to him and direct his charge at him. Should neither of the two men drive at him, the defensive man should continue on his original course. In either case, the defensive lineman should hit the opponent attacking him hard enough to keep him away from his body so that he can maintain freedom of movement.

3. PROTECT TERRITORY. On every defensive alignment, each lineman or two linemen have a certain area or territory for which he or they are responsible. He or they must protect this area until he or they are positive that the offensive play has not been directed in their territory.

Defensive linemen who look into the backfield rather than key the offensive linemen in their area are often misled by the faking of the backs, as to where the offensive play has been directed. A defensive lineman who has the tendency to look into the backfield is usually defeated by the offensive blocker since he will not see the movement of the offensive men in his area and, therefore, will not be able to react to them.

By keying the offensive linemen, in their area, the defensive linemen usually are able to know whether or not the offensive play is to be directed at them.

In order to clarify this point, let's take as an example, the two defensive guards on a normal six man line. Their assignment is to line up head up with the offensive guards two feet off the line of scrimmage. As the ball is snapped, charge hard straight into the guards being sure that you are never blocked to the outside by the guards or center. They are responsible for the territory between them.

On a trap play to the right between the two guards, the center would block the right defensive guard. The right offensive guard would influence the left defensive guard and the left offensive guard would pull and block the left defensive guard (*Illustration #1*).

ILLUSTRATION #1.

If the guards are keying the linemen in their area properly, they will react to the inside to protect their territory (*Illustration #2*). The backfield maneuver on this play has the two halfbacks and fullbacks start to their right. The quarterback reverse pivots faking a wide pitchout to the right halfback. He then turns back and gives the ball to the left halfback who runs between the two guards (*Illustration #3*).

If the defensive left guard were looking into the backfield and not keying the offensive linemen in his area, he would probably move to the outside allowing himself to *be blocked out* by the left offensive guard.

The play would undoubtedly be successful since the left guard did not protect his territory. By moving to the outside and allowing himself to be blocked further to the outside, he created a hole too wide for the right defensive guard to cover had the right guard played it properly.

ILLUSTRATION #2.

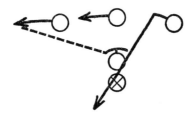

ILLUSTRATION #3.

4. PURSUE. The first objective of the defense is not to permit the opponent to score. Defensive teams that can prevent the "easy touchdown" are difficult to score against and they are seldom defeated. The forcing unit of any defense must keep this uppermost in mind.

It is possible to prevent the long "easy touchdown" if the forcing unit will react quickly on the proper side of the angle of pursuit after each man has protected his own territory.

The most vital single phase of the forcing unit's defensive play is to adjust to the proper angle of pursuit on every offensive play. On each play, each man must first protect his territory and then move to the ball. The course on which he moves is at an angle which will put him in front of the ball carrier at the earliest possible moment.

When he gets to the ball carrier, he must be able to make the tackle. All of his efforts will have been in vain if he misses the tackle.

5. MAKE THE TACKLE. All defensive men must be able to execute the fundamental of tackling. An offensive play is not completed until the ball carrier has been tackled. To have had a good stance; to have charged on the snap of the ball and keyed properly; to have protected your territory and to have pursued on the proper angle will have all been in vain if the tackle is missed.

The factors involved in the area of contact to make a good tackle are:

1. A good base—feet the width of the shoulders.
2. Knees flexed—to be able to uncoil and lift.
3. Eyes on the target—the ball.

To execute a good tackle, the man making the tackle should, with his forehead directed at the ball, drive his head through the ball. By directing his forehead rather than the top of his head at the ball, he will be able to keep his eyes on his target and react to it.

By driving his head through the ball, one thing is insured. Since the ball is carried on one side or the other of the ball carrier, the head will just clear the body of the ball carrier when the forehead is aimed at the ball. This will insure the tackler a solid shoulder rather than an arm tackle.

Another reason for the tackler to drive his head through the ball is that if he does successfully hit the ball, the ball may be driven out of the hands of the ball carrier and a fumble will result. One of the basic objectives of the defense is to force the offense to fumble.

As the tackler drives his head through the ball, he should continue to move towards the ball carrier and make contact with his shoulder.

As the contact is made, the tackler should surround the ball carrier with both arms and grab his pants or jersey. At the same time, he should lift the ball carrier off the ground using all of the muscles in his legs and back. The ball carrier will lose his forward drive as soon as his feet are no longer in contact with the ground. At this point, the tackler will be able to drive through the ball carrier knocking him backward. The ball carrier should end up on his back on the ground with the tackler on top of him. A tackler should never allow a ball carrier to fall forward.

CHAPTER THIRTEEN

Defensive Fundamentals
and Techniques

To be able to execute the fundamentals required of a defensive lineman, a player must have a good stance which will enable him to charge quickly while defending himself against an opponent.

In most circumstances, a defensive lineman will line up approximately 18 inches away from an offensive lineman. His opponent knows the starting count and will probably beat him to the charge. If the defensive man has an awkward, unbalanced stance, his opponent will be able to move the 18 inches and get contact before he can recover his balance from a bad stance. Therefore, it is absolutely essential that a defensive lineman has a good sound stance in every detail. A good defensive stance will vary with the physical build of individuals.

1. DEFENSIVE STANCE FOR LINEMEN. Basically, a good defensive stance is similar to that of a good offensive stance. The position of the feet being the difference. In assuming a defensive defense, a lineman should spread his feet slightly wider than the width of his shoulders. His feet should be staggered with the inside foot being dropped back so that the toe is even with the heel of the opposite foot. Linemen playing on the right side of the defensive line should drop their left foot back; linemen on the left side should drop their right foot back.

The weight should be equally distributed on the feet so that balance is even between both feet. A defensive man must be able to step with either foot first.

The hand corresponding to the rear foot should be placed on the ground 5 or 6 inches in front of the shoulder and just inside of the foot which is dropped back. With the hand on the ground, the lineman should bend the knees so that the back will be parallel to the ground. From this position, the feet should be moved back 6 or 8 inches, using the same stagger. Enough weight should then be placed in the hand so that if it is lifted from the ground, the lineman would fall forward. With weight forward, the defensive linemen will be able to charge forward quickly on the snap of the ball to meet the offensive blockers.

The middle of the forearm of the other arm should be placed slightly above the corresponding knee. This will cause the shoulders to be parallel to the line of scrimmage and the ground which is essential in a good stance. From this position, the hand and forearm can be moved forward quickly for block protection of the corresponding leg.

The head must be up so that the line of vision is parallel to the ground. This will enable the player to see not only the opponent in front of him, but also the players on either side of him. It is imperative that he is able to see all three of his opponents since he must key and react to their movements.

A good defensive stance is one from which a player can react with a forward movement with the snap of the ball. If he can react quickly and be moving at the time contact is made with the offensive man, there is a greater possibility that he can maintain freedom of movement and avoid the block.

2. ALIGNMENT. Defensive alignments pertain to the position where a player lines up on defense. Proper defensive alignment is of paramount importance. Unless the defensive man lines up accurately, it is impossible for him to execute his assignment.

Defensive linemen may line up head on, shade one side or the other, or play on the inside or outside shoulder of an offensive lineman. He may also line up on or off the line of scrimmage. There are many methods of teaching alignments, such as, eye on eye, nose on nose, or nose on ear. All these methods have been used successfully. However, alignment by feet position has given our defensive linemen a more accurate alignment to execute their defensive assignment.

It has been our experience that linemen line up more accurately when they line up according to feet position. To clarify this, let us take a few examples.

a. To shade the inside, the defensive lineman would line up with his outside foot just inside the outside foot of the offensive lineman.

b. To shade the outside, the defensive player would line up with his inside foot just outside the inside foot of the offensive man.

c. To line up on the outside shoulder, the defensive man would line up with his inside foot splitting the width of the offensive man's stance.

d. To line up on the inside shoulder, the player would line up with his outside foot splitting the stance of the offensive man.

Whether a defensive lineman should line up on the line of scrimmage or off the line of scrimmage depends on his defensive assignment. Should his assignment be to line up on the inside shoulder of the offensive lineman and control his outside, it would be impossible to execute this assignment if the defensive linemen would line up on the line of scrimmage. To control the outside of an offensive lineman when lined up on the inside shoulder, the defensive man must line up at least eighteen (18) inches off the line of scrimmage.

The various distances a defensive lineman should line up off the line of scrimmage will be covered under defensive charges. It is understood that these distances will vary with the individual player. There is, however, a basic rule all defensive linemen should remember. Whenever a defensive lineman is being defeated constantly, he should move back off the line of scrimmage. This will give him more time to react to the movement of the offensive players in his area and will enable him to use his block protection on the proper man and avoid being blocked.

3. BLOCK PROTECTION. Defensive linemen must maintain freedom of movement. By keeping the legs free, one will have the ability to retain freedom of movement. Block protection is the ability to protect oneself, with his hands, arms and shoulders from

an offensive blocker. As long as the legs are free, the body can move.

Four types of block protection defensive linemen can use to protect themselves are (1) hand shiver, (2) forearm lift, (3) forearm block, and (4) arm lift. It is not likely that any one player can perfect all four types. However, a player can develop and use at least two types. The block protections used would depend on the physical build of the individual player. The short and compact player would probably use the hand shiver and the forearm lift. He would probably use them more effectively because he would be able to use his hands and forearms forcefully and still stay low enough so that his legs would not be vulnerable for a block.

The tall defensive player would probably use the forearm lift and arm lift more effectively as it would be difficult for him to stay low enough to use the hand shiver.

The average height player could probably use all four types of block protection. He should, however, only use the ones he can perfect and use effectively.

The type of block protection used by a player will also depend on his defensive assignment. Should his assignment be to control an offensive man, protecting the area to either side of his opponent, he would use a hand shiver. This type of block protection would enable him to protect himself from the offensive linemen on either side of the man he is controlling.

Should his assignment be to control the outside of an offensive lineman from a head-on alignment, he would use either a forearm lift or a forearm block with his inside arm. This would enable him to protect himself with his outside arm against the offensive blocker outside of the player whose outside he is controlling.

Should he be assigned to control the outside of the offensive man from an inside shoulder alignment, he would use the arm lift with his inside arm. This would give him more protection for his legs as he moves laterally to the outside and would also give him his outside arm for protection against anyone outside who may be attempting to block him.

Hand Shiver. To execute the hand shiver, the defensive man should step forward with his rear foot bringing it even with the opposite foot. At the same time, the heels of the hands should be directed at a spot just under the shoulders of the offensive blocker. The body should be uncoiled and the hands and arms should be extended sharply. As contact is made, the hands should be driven up. This will raise the offensive blocker up and cause this center of gravity to be higher than the defensive player's. The defensive player will now be able to keep the offensive lineman away from his body and maintain freedom of movement. He will have the ability to move laterally with the ball carrier.

Forearm Lift. The forearm lift is executed in much the same manner. The difference being that it is delivered with one arm rather than both hands. The inside arm being used when controlling the outside and the outside arm being employed when controlling inside.

A short step forward should be taken with the foot corresponding to the arm which is being used. The forearm should be directed at the numerals on the jersey of the offensive man. As the step is taken, the body should be uncoiled and the forearm driven into the offensive man. The opposite hand should be used as added protection by driving it just under the shoulder of the offensive player. As contact is made, the defensive man should follow through with the forearm, raising up the opponent and keeping him away from his body. This will enable the defensive man to control the offensive man, and allow him to move laterally to the ball.

Forearm Block. The forearm block is used primarily when a defensive man is controlling the outside of an offensive lineman from a shading the outside position and is executed in the same manner as the forearm lift. The first step (foot corresponding with the arm being used) should be taken forward on a slight outside angle. The target is the juncture of the outside shoulder and neck. As the step is taken, the forearm should be driven at the target. The defensive man should endeavor to keep the head of the offensive man inside of his forearm. By doing this, it is impossible for the offensive man to block him in. This will enable the defensive lineman to protect the area to the outside of the offensive man. The outside hand is used on the blocker should the defensive man fail with the forearm block, allowing the offensive player to get his head by his forearm.

Arm Lift. The arm lift is used primarily when the defensive man's assignment is to control the outside of an offensive man from an inside shoulder alignment. (His outside foot splitting the stance of the offensive man.) To execute this assignment, the defensive man must be at least eighteen (18) inches off the line of scrimmage.

The first step will be taken to the outside almost parallel to the line of scrimmage with the inside foot. As the step is taken, the inside arm is extended and driven between the opponent and the inside leg, protecting the leg from the offensive lineman. Should contact be made, the defensive man should follow through with the arm, raising the opponent up and keeping him away from his legs. As long as the legs are free, the body can move.

4. DEFENSIVE CHARGES. There are many different defensive alignments that may be used, but regardless of the alignments, there are only five fundamental plays that defensive linemen must be able to execute. These are: 1. control offensive man 2. control one side of an offensive man 3. penetrating charge (goal line) 4. slant charge 5. loop charge.

In executing any one of the above plays, the defensive man must keep the fundamentals for any defensive charge uppermost in his mind. They are: 1. charge on the snap of the ball 2. protect himself and his territory 3. move to the ball 4. make the tackle.

a. *Control offensive man*—when controlling an offensive man, the defensive man is responsible for the area on either side of him. He must be able to protect himself from the offensive man on either side of the man he is controlling.

To execute this play, the defensive man lines up head on the offensive man approximately two (2) feet off the line of scrimmage. This alignment will enable him to see and react to the three men in his area. By using the *hand shiver*, the defensive man will be able to direct his charge at the offensive blocker on either side should he attempt to block him. Should he use a forearm lift, he allows himself to be vulnerable to the offensive blocker on the side corresponding to the arm which he uses in executing the forearm lift.

b. *Control one side of an offensive man*—when controlling the outside or inside of an offensive lineman, the defensive player is responsible for the area to the side he is controlling. He must be able to protect himself from an offensive blocker lined up on that side of the man he is controlling.

To execute this charge, when controlling the outside of an offensive blocker, the defensive man will line up on the line of scrimmage shading the outside of the offensive man (his inside foot just outside the inside foot of the offensive man).

As he starts his charge, he will step with his inside foot, directing it just outside the middle of the offensive man's stance. He will use a forearm lift with his inside arm directing it at the chest just outside of the offensive man's head. The shoulder and arm should be on the outside of the offensive player's head. As long as the head of the offensive blocker is controlled by the defensive man's arm to the inside, he will not be able to block him in.

As contact is made, the outside foot should be adjusted to a position that will give the defensive man a good base with his outside foot back. Even though the blocker may get his head outside the defensive man's arm, it is still difficult to block him in if the defensive man has his outside foot back.

By using the technique of controlling the outside from an inside position, rather than an outside position, gives the defensive man the advantage of moving out in the direction of the area he is assigned to protect. He is, also, in a better position to see and to react to the offensive man lined up outside, from whom he must be able to protect himself with his outside arm should the offensive player attempt to block him.

To control the inside, the defensive charge would be made in the same manner by shading the inside, stepping with the outside foot, using the forearm lift with the outside arm and adjusting the inside foot.

c. *Penetrating charge (goal line)*—the basic objective of a goal line charge is to get across the line of scrimmage as quickly as possible with a low aggressive charge. This type of charge is best made from a four-point stance. In this stance, both hands are placed on the ground in the same position as the one hand in the normal defensive three-point stance. The feet should be well up in under the body, bringing them closer to the line of scrimmage. This will enable the defensive lineman to get his body across the line of scrimmage more quickly and to get further penetration as he lunges and brings his feet forward.

To execute the goal line charge, the defensive man lines up on the line of scrimmage in the gap between two offensive blockers. As the charge is made, the hands shoot forward forcing an opening. The shoulders are driven forward with a slight dipping action, attempting to get under the shoulders of the offensive blockers. As the body is extended, the feet should be brought forward as quickly as possible. As the defensive man regains his balance, he should continue to drive for further penetration.

d. *Slant Charge*—a slant charge can be used as a penetrating charge or a controlling charge.

To execute a penetrating slant right charge, the defensive man will line up on the line of scrimmage, head on an offensive lineman. As he starts his charge, he will take a fast diagonal step to his right with his left foot, followed by a fast diagonal step with his right foot directing his right shoulder at the hip of the offensive lineman to his right. He will use an arm lift with his left arm to protect his legs as he takes the diagonal steps.

As the offensive man on his right charges forward, the defensive man continues on a course that will take him to the spot of hip of the offensive man's stance. As he arrives on the spot, he must maneuver his body so that his shoulders are parallel to the line of scrimmage.

A penetrating slant left charge is executed in the same manner in the opposite direction.

To execute a controlling slant right charge, the defensive lineman will line up head on the offensive lineman approximately 1 foot off the line of scrimmage. As he starts his charge, he will take a fast diagonal step with his left foot followed by a fast diagonal step with his right foot, directing his left shoulder at the juncture of the neck and shoulder of the offensive lineman to his right.

He will use an arm lift with his left arm to protect his legs as he takes the first two steps. After his first two steps, he will have his hands ready to use a hand shiver and will react to the movement of the offensive man to his right.

A controlling slant left charge is executed in the same manner in the opposite direction.

e. *Loop Charge*—a loop charge can be used in a penetrating charge or a controlling charge.

A loop charge to penetrate can only be executed around the offensive man the defensive man is lined up on. To execute this charge to penetrate to the right, the defensive man will line up on the line of scrimmage, shading the right side of his opponent. As he starts his charge, he will take a fast diagonal step with his left foot, followed by a fast diagonal step with his right foot, directing his left shoulder just outside the offensive man. He will use a left arm lift for block protection. He should, however, try to avoid contact so that he can penetrate around his opponent, getting depth in the backfield. A loop charge to penetrate to the left is executed in the same manner in the opposite direction.

A loop charge to control is executed around the man to the left or right of the offensive man on whom the defensive man has taken his alignment. To execute a controlling loop charge to the right, the defensive man must line up a yard off the line of scrimmage, head on or shading the right side of the offensive lineman. As he starts his charge, he will take a fast lateral step with his left foot, followed by a fast lateral step with his right foot. As soon as he is past the head of the opponent to his right, he should maneuver his body so that his shoulders are parallel to the line of scrimmage. He does not attempt to penetrate, but he must get past the head of his opponent so that he can not be blocked. He must loop far enough to be in a position to protect his territory.

To loop left, the same procedure is used in the opposite direction.

LINEBACKERS

1. LINEMEN. It is essential that linebackers have a good stance. Since the offensive blockers are farther away, and the linebacker has a short interval of time after the ball is snapped to adjust his stance and assume a hitting position, it is not as necessary for a linebacker to be in a perfect stance as it is for linemen. It is, however, advantageous for a linebacker to have a good stance which will enable him to move in any direction when the play begins.

A linebacker in assuming his stance, should spread his feet approximately the width of his shoulders. Either foot may be dropped back, but no further than toe and heel. Since the linebacker will take at least two steps before making contact, it is necessary for him to drop either foot back. His feet must be in a position that will enable him to move in any direction. The knees should be flexed and his body bent slightly at the waist. The arms should be allowed to hang straight down with a slight bend at the elbows. The shoulders should be parallel to the line of scrimmage. The head should be in a position so that the line of vision is parallel to the ground. This will enable the linebacker to see his key, which in most instances will be an offensive lineman.

2. ALIGNMENT. It is vitally important that a linebacker lines up accurately. This will enable him to play with maximum efficiency. If he is out of position merely a foot or two, this small distance may mean the difference between stopping the ball carrier for no gain or allowing the ball carrier to run by him for a long gain.

A linebacker will take his lateral alignment in the same maner as that of a defensive lineman. He will line up by feet position for the various alignments, head on, shade inside, shade outside, inside shoulder and outside shoulder. His vertical alignment will vary from on the line of scrimmage to four or five yards off the line of scrimmage, depending on his assignment and down and yardage to be gained.

Should the linebacker's assignment be to delay or hold up an end, he would play in the line of scrimmage. If the offensive team had a fourth down and twelve yard situation on the twenty-five yard line going in, the linebacker would play four or five yards off the line of scrimmage. Any gain less than twelve yards would be a successful play as the offensive teams would not make the first down and would lose possession of the ball.

On every play, a linebacker must be conscious of what the offense must accomplish to maintain possession of the ball. This is the most important single factor in playing tactically sound defense.

3. KEYING. In practice drills, most linebackers watch the proper man and key well. However, when they work in team defense, many men forget about their key and watch the opponent's backfield. Linebackers must discipline themselves to play their key in every situation.

A linebacker must be able to react to his key. There are occasions when his key may be a man in the backfield, however, in most instances, it will be an offensive lineman. By the movement of this lineman, the linebacker will know immediately whether the play is a pass or run. If the play is a run, the movement of this lineman will indicate the direction the run will develop.

There are six basic movements which a lineman can make. These are: (1.) charge at the linebacker, (2.) block the lineman to his right, (3.) block the lineman to his left, (4.) pull to the right, (5.) pull to the left, and (6.) drop back for pass protection.

The linebacker should react to each key in the following manner: (1.) If the lineman charges at him, he should move forward and meet the lineman with a forearm lift or hand shiver, control him, protect his territory, move to the ball and make the tackle. (2.) If the lineman blocks either to his right or left, the linebacker should move forward on an angle to the side of the block, closing the hole. He should not penetrate across the line of scrimmage. (3.) If the lineman pulls to either side, the linebacker should go with him. (4.) If the lineman makes a pass protection block, the linebacker should drop back on the proper angle to the hook-pass zone.

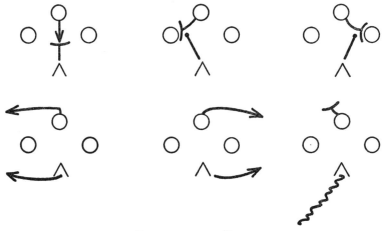

ILLUSTRATION #1.

If a linebacker can learn to make these reactions quickly and accurately as the offensive lineman moves, he will be in a position to support almost every play. Learning to key properly, without taking a false-step or a step in the wrong direction, is simply a matter of practice in reacting to the movement of an offensive player.

4. *Play Versus Run.* When a linebacker's key indicates a run, he must first protect his territory and then move to the ball. The course on which he moves is the angle of pursuit. He must move at the angle which will put him in front of the ball carrier at the earliest possible moment.

On every running play, some member of the offensive team will attempt to block the linebacker. In protecting himself, the linebacker should use a forearm lift or hand shiver in the same manner as defensive lineman. Since the linebacker is in an up-right stance as he reacts to his key, he must adjust to the hitting position in the area of contact. He must lower his center of gravity and flex his knees as he delivers the forearm lift or hand shiver. The blow should be delivered from underneath his opponent and should raise him up, keeping the blocker away from his body so that he can continue to move to the ball. When he gets to the ball carrier, he must be able to make the tackle. All of his efforts will have been in vain if he misses the tackle.

5. *Play Versus Pass.* When the linebacker's key indicates pass, he must react quickly and drop back fast on the correct angle to the proper spot.

There is a great deal of discussion among coaches as to which is the best and fastest way for a linebacker to drop to the hook zone. We have found that linebackers can best get to the spot by simply running backwards. This also enables the linebacker to watch the passer as he is dropping back.

As the linebacker drops back, if any receiver starts across the field in front of him, he should step forward and hit him with a forearm lift or hand shiver. The linebacker should never allow any receiver across the field unless he goes deep behind him. He should hit and slow up any receiver who comes close enough to him to be touched.

By watching the passer intently, actually studying his face and his eyes, the proper reaction to the throw of the ball can be developed. The linebacker must move to the ball as the passer starts to throw. If he waits until he releases the ball, he will always be too late. When the ball is in the air, the linebacker must remember it belongs to him and always try for the interception.

CHAPTER FOURTEEN

Assignments and Responsibilities of the Forcing Unit

A defensive quarterback must know the tactical situation to be able to put his team in the proper defense. To be able to play the defense intelligently, each defensive player must also be aware of the tactical situation on every single down.

There are six items which govern offensive tactics. These are: (1) score, (2) time, (3) weather, (4) down, (5) yardage and (6) field position. The changing of any one of the six will change the tactical situation. For example: (1) Score — If a team is ahead, they will call safer plays and will not gamble as much as they will when they are behind. (2) Time — If a team is behind with a minute to play, they will call plays differently than if they were behind with 45 minutes to play. (3) Weather — If there is a wind blowing strongly against the offense, they are not likely to pass. Also, they usually will not kick the ball until forced to do so. When an offensive team has the wind at their backs, exactly the reverse is true. (4) Down — The offensive team will usually call a different play on 4th down and ten than they will on first and ten. (5) Yardage — If the offensive team must make fifteen yards on one play, they usually will call a different play than if they need to make only a half a yard. (6) Field Position — If the offense has the ball deep in their own territory, they will usually play conservatively. As they move downfield, they usually open up their attack. Some teams also call different types of plays when they are on the hashmark with wide field to their right or wide field to their left than when they do from the middle of the field.

Depending on the type of defense being used, each of the players in the forcing unit has a specific assignment and responsibilities on every play. The forcing unit of any team defense must have a draw man, screen men, and leverage men. The draw man is responsible for the draw play from a fake drop back pass. The screen men are responsible for a screen pass to their side. The leverage men are responsible for keeping the ball inside of them. The three types of leverage plays are: (1) play at the leverage man, (2) reverse and (3) pass.

When a play is directed at the leverage man, he must never get as deep as the ball where he can be blocked out and enable the ball carrier to run a straight course to the outside. He must stay at least a yard and a half in front of the ball and not allow the blocker to block him in. He must move to the outside on an angle which will enable him to either force the ball carrier out of bounds or tackle him for a gain of not more than three yards. Should a deep, delayed reverse be directed at the leverage man, he should get as deep as the ball and force the ball carrier to run inside.

If the play is a pass, the two leverage men must keep outside leverage on the passer and force him to run inside should he decide, or be forced, to run with the ball.

A responsibility of the forcing unit is to control the splits of the offensive line. Certain defensive players, they may be linebackers or linemen, are assigned to cut down the splits of the guards, tackles and ends. Should they be unable to accomplish this, any time the split between the two offensive men is large enough, the player responsible for that split will move in and shoot the gap. The defensive player will take his alignment on the line of scrimmage just inside half the distance of the split and on the snap of the ball, charge for penetration.

The two basic alignments used by the forcing units as played by the University of Oklahoma are: (1) an odd alignment with a box secondary and (2) an even alignment with a three deep secondary. The odd alignment consists of four men in the containing unit and seven men in the forcing unit. The even alignment played will normally have five men in the containing unit and six men in the forcing unit.

The odd alignment of the forcing unit will be able to force the issue better than the even alignment. The even alignment having one more man in the containing unit would be able to contain the defensive team better. However, in the even alignment, the defensive ends (normally in the containing unit) may be used in the forcing portion. The three remaining men in the containing unit will probably not be able to contain the offense quite as well, but the eight men in the forcing unit will do an adequate job of making a real issue at the line of scrimmage with the offensive team.

Several basic alignments can be used with the seven men of a forcing unit in the box defense. The most normal set-ups are: (1) A five-two, (2) a six-one, (3) a four-three, and (4) a seven-man line.

The same is true with the six men in the forcing unit when five men are in the containing unit. It must be remembered that the defensive ends of the containing portion may be used in the forcing unit. The standard alignments for the eight men are: (1) a six-two, (2) a five-three, (3) a seven-one, and (4) a four-four.

From each of the basic alignments in both forcing units, there are a variety of alignments which may be employed. They are used to attempt to confuse the offensive line in regards to their blocking assignments.

This will be covered in greater length later. Briefly, this can be done by over-shifting a few defensive linemen a half a man and under-shifting the linebackers to compensate for the over-shift of the linemen.

Regardless of the various alignments used by the forcing unit, each player will have a definite assignment—an area to protect. A player will be responsible for the draw play, two will be leverage men and two men will be responsible for the screen pass.

Defense 72, a 5:4:2 alignment, which is known universally as the "Oklahoma Defense", is one of the two basic defenses used at the University of Oklahoma. *(Illustration #1.)*

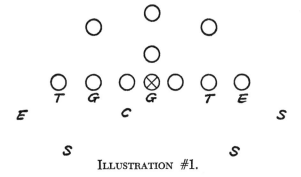

ILLUSTRATION #1.

The assignments and responsibilities of the individual players in the forcing unit are as follows:

Left Tackle and Right End: Line up shading the outside of the offensive end. Your assignment is to control his outside. As the ball is snapped, charge hard into the end being sure that the end is not able to block you in. (This alignment and the execution of the defensive charge is explained in detail in Chapter 13, Defensive Fundamentals and Techniques.) Key and react to the end.

1. If the end attempts to block you in, give ground quickly along the line of scrimmage to the outside. The end must never block you in.
2. If the end blocks to the inside, do not penetrate. Move to the inside and close the gap. Be ready to plan an inside out block by a lineman.
3. If the end attempts to block you out, fight the pressure. Attempt to close the hole to the inside by giving a little ground and force the end in to close the hole. Keep the end to your inside.
4. If the end attempts to go downfield, hold him on the line of scrimmage as long as you can.

You are the leverage men.

1. If the ball comes your way, stay 1½ to 2 yards in front of the ball. Meet the blockers, give ground to outside and maintain leverage on the ball. Keep it in front of you until you can make the tackle or force the ball carrier out of bounds.

2. When the end does get away from you and the ball has started in the opposite direction, penetrate across the line of scrimmage. Get as deep as the ball and force the play. You have leverage on reverse plays.

3. When the end gets away from you and a drop back pass develops, you have leverage on the passer and are repsonsible for screen passes to your side. Do not allow the passer out of the pocket. Should he be forced to run, make him run up the middle.

You are responsible for the split between the end and the tackle. Whenever the split is large enough, move in and shoot the gap.

Your adjustments to split ends and flankers are:

1. If your end splits, move in to your normal position, penetrate, go to the ball.

2. If your end splits and any back lines up inside of the end, play the back as an end. Your normal rules are the same. If the back lines up in the normal distance of the end, play on him. If he lines up wide, move in and shoot the gap.

On unbalanced offensive alignments, line up on the end man on the line of scrimmage. These alignments may have four or five men on one side of the center and the remaining men on the other side.

Left Guard and Right Tackle: Line up shading the outside of the offensive tackle. Your assignment is to control the outside of him. As the ball is snapped, charge hard into the tackle being sure that he cannot block you in. You are responsible for any play directed between you and your defensive man over the end. Key and react to the tackle and end.

1. Be ready to play the double team block by the end.

2. If the tackle blocks to the inside, do not penetrate. Move to the inside and close the gap, keep the tackle to your inside.

3. If the tackle pulls to the outside, play first for the trap from the inside. If it is not the trap play, go to the ball.

4. If the tackle makes a pass protection block, rush the passer.

5. If your tackle gets away from you and moves downfield, move up quickly on the proper angle of pursuit to get in front of the ball carrier at the earliest possible moment. You are responsible for the split between the tackle and guard. On unbalanced offensive alignments, move one man to the unbalanced side on a 4:2 alignment and two men on a 5:1 alignment.

Right Guard: Line up head up with the offensive center approximately 2 to 2½ feet off the line of scrimmage. You must be in a position to key and react to the center and the two offensive guards. Your assignment is to control the center (Refer to Chapter 13, A Control Charge). You must never allow the center to cut you either way. You must control both sides of the center, maintain your ability to move to either side.

If you line up on the line of scrimmage, the center will be able to block you either way. If you charge hard on every play, you can be cut to one side or the other more easily by the center. If you take a controlled charge, it will be difficult for the center to take you either way. This charge cannot be taken too softly or the center will be able to knock you back.

A little variance in the strength of your charge will make it more difficult for the center to block you as he cannot anticipate the type of charge you will use. About one out of four or five plays, charge hard and attempt to knock the center straight back. Key and react to the center and both offensive guards.

1. Be ready to direct your charge into either guard should he attempt to block you.
2. If the three men make pass protection blocks, play first for the draw play. You are responsible for the draw play. After you are sure it is not a draw play, rush the passer.
3. If the play is directed away from your area, locate the ball and pursue on the proper angle. On unbalanced offensive alignments, move one man to the unbalanced side on a 4:2 alignment and two men on a 5:1 alignment.

The right guard has the most difficult defensive assignment of the forcing unit since he must control both sides of one offensive man. Against an equally capable opponent, this is a very difficult assignment. All the other men in the forcing unit are assigned to protect one side of an offensive lineman which enables the defense to hold up adequately.

Linebackers: Line up a yard and a half off the line of scrimmage shading the outside of the offensive guard. Your assignment is to control the outside of the guard.

1. If the guard drives out at you, charge into him being sure he cannot block you in. You are responsible first for any play directed between you and your defensive man on your outside.

2. If the guard blocks to his inside or outside, move forward quickly on a slight angle to the side of the power block. Do not cross the line of scrimmage. When the guard blocks in on the man over center, be ready to play the trap block by the opposite guard. If, as you move forward, you close the gap between you and the middle defensive guard and do not penetrate, the trap blocker will find it difficult to make a satisfactory block. If the guard blocks out, be ready to play a block from the outside in by the halfback.

3. If the guard pulls in either direction, move with the guard, locate the ball, and pursue on the proper angle. If the guard pulls to the inside, play first for the trap before pursuing.

4. If the guard makes a pass protection block, move quietly on the proper angle to the hook zone and play the ball.

From this forcing unit alignment, several stunts may be used to attempt to create the "Six Yard Situation" (the offensive team must average six yards a play to make a first down). The basic stunts are cross-charges by the linebackers with the linemen head on the tackle and center *(Illustration #2, Stunt #1)*.

ILLUSTRATION #2, STUNT #1.

1. On the first stunt, the linemen lined up on the offensive tackle executes a penetrating slant charge to the inside *(*refer to Chapter XIII, *Penetrating Slant Charge)* while the linebackers shoot the gap over the position of the defensive linemen were originally lined up. This stunt can be executed on both sides at the same time or independently on either side.

Left Guard and Right Tackle: Line up exactly as you do on Regular Defense 72. Your assignment is to execute a penetrating slant charge to the inside. You are responsible for any play directed outside the offensive guard and inside your linebacker. Key and react to the guard as you make your charge.

1. If the guard blocks out on you, attempt to flatten your course, staying close to the line of scrimmage.
2. If the guard blocks the middle guard, play for the trap.
3. If the guard pulls out of the line either way, adjust to a shallow course and follow him; he will take you to the ball.
4. If the guard makes a pass protection block, rush the passer. If the guard blocks straight ahead, penetrate on your slant charge and get to the ball as fast as possible.

Linebackers: Line up in your normal position on Defense 72. As the guard charges, taking your first step with your far foot, shoot the gap directly over his original position. Your assignment is to control the outside of the tackle should he block you. You are responsible for any play directed outside of the offensive tackle between you and the defensive man over the end. Key and react to the movement of the tackle as you shoot.

1. The tackle will normally be blocking on the lineman and you will be able to penetrate quickly into the backfield. As you shoot, adjust quickly to the course of the ball. If it is coming your way, do not over-run the play. If the ball is going away, adjust rapidly and move with it.
2. If the tackle is dropping back for a pass protection block, rush the passer.

The second stunt involved the middle guard and the linebackers *(Illustration #3).*

ILLUSTRATION #3.

If the middle guard and the left linebacker are executing the stunt, the middle guard executes a penetrating slant charge to his left. He keys and reacts to the offensive guard in the same manner the defensive left guard on right tackle did in Stunt Number One. As the middle guard makes his charge, the left linebacker must shoot the gap quickly over the spot where the offensive center was lined up.

A third stunt has the two defensive linemen and linebacker on one side of the line shooting through the gap to their outside. If a wide play has been called, this defensive stunt is most effective. The stunt is executed only on one side and usually to the side of the wide field (*Illustration #4*).

ILLUSTRATION #4.

It is executed as follows:

Left Tackle and Left Guard or Right End and Right Tackle: Line up exactly as you would for regular Defense 72. Your assignment is to execute a penetrating loop charge to the outside (Refer to Chapter 13, Penetrating Loop Charge). Be sure your offensive man does not block you in. Having penetrated, react quickly to the ball.

Linebackers: Line up exactly as you would on regular Defense 72. As the ball is snapped, execute a penetrating loop charge to the outside of the offensive guard. React quickly to the ball.

When this stunt is employed, the middle guard should protect the side of the stunt so that he will be in position to stop the play if it were directed between the offensive center and the offensive guard.

There are several alignments which may be used from the basic 5:2 odd alignment. The assignments and responsibilities would remain relatively the same. One of these alignments can be accomplished by off-setting the middle guard either way, in the gap between the center and guard. Position the linebacker to the side the guard is off-set, directly behind the guard. The other five men play their normal positions and assignments (*Illustration #5*).

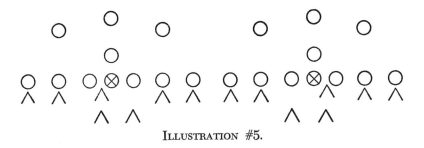

ILLUSTRATION #5.

From this alignment, the guard and linebacker can cross-charge either way (*Illustration #6*).

ILLUSTRATION #6.

The guard can attempt to penetrate through the gap and the linebacker key and react to the offensive guard. Should the guard block down on the defensive guard, the linebacker would shoot the gap outside the guard. Should the guard drive at the linebacker, he would move to the inside and play the ball. He would react normally to all other movements (*Illustration #7*).

ILLUSTRATION #7.

Another alignment can be employed by off-setting the defensive men on the tackles in the inside gap. The linebackers may line up on the offensive tackle or may be positioned directly behind the linemen in the gap (*Illustration #8*).

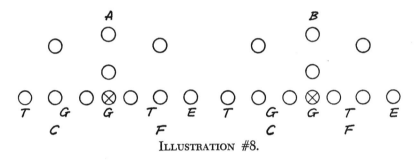

ILLUSTRATION #8.

From either alignment, the two linemen and linebackers may cross-charge in the same manner as the middle guard and linebacker in *Illustration #6*. Another type of stunt which is very effective from Alignment "A" is to slant the three middle linemen either way and shoot the linebacker away from the slant. The other linebacker takes one step away from the slant and keys and reacts to the guard. To execute the slant to the left, the middle guard takes a penetrating slant charge to his left; the left guard and tackle execute a penetrating loop charge to their left (Refer to Chapter 13, *Penetrating Loop and Slant Charge*). The left tackle and right end play their normal assignments (*Illustration #9*).

The same stunt can be executed from Alignment "B" with the two linebackers taking one step in the opposite direction of the slant keying and reacting to their offensive guards as they move.

<small>ILLUSTRATION #9.</small>

It should be kept in mind that when stunts are used within the forcing unit, the pursuit of the defensive team is somewhat impaired. If the stunts are successful, the linemen or linebackers will be able to penetrate and may tackle the ball carrier for a loss. It is possible they may even force a fumble. However, if the play is directed away from the stunt, the stunting players will be moving away from the ball. They will have to stop and adjust back to their normal angle of pursuit. Their stunt will have moved them farther away from the ball than their controlling charge on the line of scrimmage. Consequently, they will not be able to pursue quite as effectively.

These odd alignments for the forcing unit, with the stunts, are very good against an inside running attack. However, these alignments lack basic strength versus the wide option run or pass plays.

Defense 60, a 6:2:2:1 Wide Tackle alignment is the other basic defense played by the University of Oklahoma (*Illustration #10*).

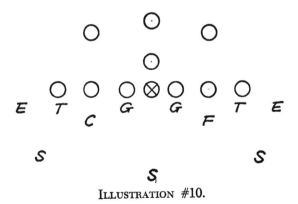

<small>ILLUSTRATION #10.</small>

The alignments, assignments and responsibilities of the individuals in the forcing unit are as follows:

Ends: Line up on the line of scrimmage 2 to 2½ feet outside the offensive end. Your assignment is to key and react to the ball. As the ball is snapped, take one step across the line of scrimmage.

1. If the ball comes your way, continue across the line of scrimmage and keep the ball about 1½ to 2 yards deeper than you are. You are responsible for maintaining leverage on the ball when it comes your way. This same reaction was described for the left tackle on the 5:2 alignment. The difference being that the end is executing deeper in the backfield as he has gone across the line of scrimmage. The end will meet the blockers in the backfield; the left tackle will meet the blockers on the line of scrimmage.

2. If the ball goes away from you, drop back quickly. You are responsible for the coverage on the deep outside on any pass play.

3. If a drop back pass develops, drop off quickly on the proper angle and cover the flat zone to your side.

Adjustments to Split Ends and Flankered Backs:

1. If the offensive end splits three yards, line up head up with him. Do not permit him to release off the line of scrimmage to the inside. Play the ball normally.

2. If the end splits more than three yards, drop off the line of scrimmage to the outside. Line up inside of the end in a position shallow enough so that the end cannot cross in front of you to catch a quick pass.

3. Adjust the same way to any flankered backs and react normally.

Tackles: Line up 18 inches off the line of scrimmage on the inside shoulder of the offensive end. Your assignment is to control the outside of the end (this alignment and the execution of the defensive charge is explained in detail in Chapter 13, Defensive Fundamentals and Techniques). As the ball is snapped, charge hard at the head of the offensive end, being sure he cannot block you in. Hold him on the line of scrimmage as long as possible. You are responsible for any play directed just outside of the offensive end. You are the leverage man on deep reverses and drop back passes. You are responsible for the screen pass to your side. The play of the leverage man on these plays was described for the left tackle and right end on the 5:2 alignment. You are responsible for the splits between the end and tackle. Whenever the split is large enough, move in and shoot the gap.

On unbalanced offensive alignments, line up on the end man on the line of scrimmage.

The adjustments to split ends and flankered backs are exactly the same as the left tackle on the 5:2 alignment.

Guards: Line up head up with the offensive guards two feet off the line of scrimmage. Your assignment is to control the offensive guard being sure that the guards are never able to block you to the outside. Key and react to the three offensive men in your area (the guard, center and tackle). You are responsible for the trap play between you. As you control the guards, locate the ball, react quickly on the proper angle of pursuit.

The right guard is responsible for the draw play.

On unbalanced offensive alignments, move one man to the unbalanced side on a 4:2 (four men on one side of the center and two on the other side) and two men on a 5:1 alignment.

Linebackers: Line up a yard and a half behind the line of scrimmage on the outside shoulder of the offensive tackle. Key and react to the tackle exactly as you do the guard on Defense 72.

1. If the tackle drives out at you, charge into him being sure he cannot block you in. You are responsible for the area between you and your defensive man on your outside.

2. If the tackle blocks to either side, move forward quickly on a slight angle to the side of the power block. Do not cross the line of scrimmage. If the tackle blocks in on the guard, be ready to play the trap block by the opposite guard. If the tackle blocks out on the tackle, be ready to play the block by the halfback.

3. If the tackle pulls either way, go with him.

4. If the tackle makes a pass protection block, drop quickly on the proper angle to the hook zone and play for the ball.

You are responsible for the split between the guard and tackle. On unbalanced offensive alignments, move one man to the unbalanced side on a 4:2 (four men on one side of the center and two on the other side) and two men on a 5:1 alignment.

Several stunts may be also used by the forcing unit from this even alignment in an attempt to create the "Six Yard Situation" or to force the fumble. Two of the basic stunts are between the linebackers and the guards or tackles (*Illustration #11, Stunt #1 Outside*).

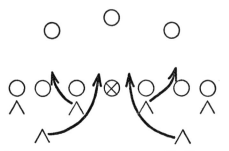

ILLUSTRATION #11, STUNT #1 OUTSIDE.

The guards take their normal alignment and on the snap of the ball execute a pentrating slant charge to the outside. The linebackers line up normally and on the snap of the ball, shoot the gap between the offensive guard on his side and the center. The linebacker should key the tackle as he shoots. If the movement of the tackle indicates that the play is directed outside, the linebackers should not go through with their stunt. They should react back to the outside on a normal angle of pursuit. The tackles and ends line up normally and execute their regular assignments. This stunt can be executed on both sides at the same time or independently on either side (*Illustration #12, Stunt #2 Inside*).

The tackles line up normally and on the snap of the ball, execute a penetrating slant charge to the inside. As they charge, they key the tackle. They react to the tackle in the same manner as the guards on stunt #1 from the 5:2 alignment. If the tackle turns out on him, he must attempt to flatten his charge so that he can-

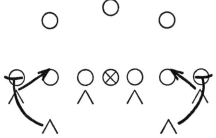

ILLUSTRATION #12, STUNT #2 INSIDE.

not be blocked out. He has the same leverage responsibilities as he does on regular Defense 60.

The linebackers line up normally and on the snap of the ball, charge hard to the outside at the offensive ends. The linebackers must hit the ends, attempting to knock them back and hold them up. They must never allow the ends to block them in. They must always release the ends to the inside. They are responsible for a play directed just outside the offensive end. After playing the end as described, they react on their normal angle of pursuit.

The linebacker must key normally and if the movement of the tackle indicates that the play is directed to the opposite side, he must react in the same manner as he does on Stunt #1 (Outside). The guards and ends line up normally and play regular Defense 60.

This stunt can be executed independently or on both sides at the same time.

Another stunt from this alignment, which is very effective is executed by the tackles and ends (*Illustration #13, Stunt #3 Crash*).

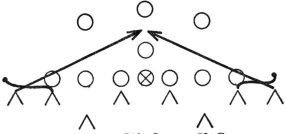

ILLUSTRATION #13, STUNT #3 CRASH.

On this stunt, the ends, on the snap of the ball, charge through the hip of the tackle for a spot one yard behind the quarterback. They react to the quarterback as they force the play as hard as possible. They have leverage on drop back passes and reverses. The tackles, on the snap of the ball, execute a control loop charge (Refer to Chapter 13) to position themselves where the ends were lined up. They then key the ball and react exactly as the end does on regular Defense 60.

The entire line and linebackers are employed in the next two stunts *(Illustration #14, Stunt #4 Tight)*.

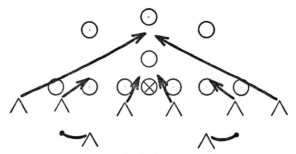

ILLUSTRATION #14, STUNT #4 TIGHT.

All players take their normal alignment. The ends charge hard for a spot one yard in front of the fullback. They must force the play and keep leverage on the fullback. They have leverage on drop back passes and reverses.

The tackles execute a penetrating slant charge to the inside and force the play. The guards shoot the gap between the guards and center and react to the play. The linebackers take one step to the outside. As the linebackers move to the outside, they key and react to the offensive tackle *(Illustration #15, Stunt #5, Rush)*.

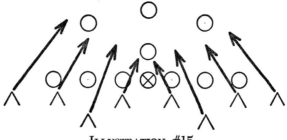

ILLUSTRATION #15.

All men line up in the regular 60 Defense alignment.

Ends: Charge hard at the outside shoulder of the offensive half-back. Keep outside leverage on the halfback if he flares. If he hits in, keep leverage on the fullback. You are responsible for the screens and have leverage on passes and reverses.

Tackles: Shoot the gap between the end and tackle directing your charge at the halfback. Force the play.

Guards: Shoot the gap between the guards and center and force the play.

Linebackers: As the ball is snapped, shoot the gap between the tackle and guard. Force the play.

Another defensive alignment which may be employed when using a 6:2 forcing unit is the tackle cross-charge. The only real adjustment involves the tackles and linebackers. The guards and ends line up and play exactly as they do on regular Defense 60 (*Illustration #16, Tackle Cross Charge 60*).

ILLUSTRATION #16.

The defensive tackle lines up 18 inches off the line of scrimmage in the gap between the offensive end and tackle. The linebacker takes his position directly behind the tackle.

The tackle and linebacker have three different plays they can execute:

1. The tackle can charge to his left and the linebacker to his right, or
2. The tackle can charge to his right and the linebacker to his left.

3. The tackle can charge straight ahead as the linebacker keys the offensive end and tackle.

The tackle will use a controlling slant charge when playing the tackle or end (Refer to Chapter 13). The linebacker will charge the end or tackle, whichever is his assignment, exactly as he charges the end on 60 Stunt #2 Inside *(Illustration #17)*.

ILLUSTRATION #17.

When the tackle shoots through the gap, the linebacker keys and reacts to the end and tackle. If either the end or tackle block the shooting tackle, the linebacker will fill to that side. If the end blocks, the linebacker will move to the outside. If the tackle blocks, the linebacker will move to the inside. If neither block the tackle, he will penetrate and be in a position to stop the ball carrier should the play be directed at him.

With the exception of defense, kicking is the most important single phase. The forcing unit of the defense is responsible for rushing the kicker in an attempt to block the kick. If the unit is not successful in blocking the kick, it should force the punter to hurry his kick. This will cause the punter to get away a shorter kick, giving the ball to the forcing unit's team in a more favorable field position.

It is also the responsibility of the forcing unit to form a punt-return pattern. On a surekick situation, whether the forcing unit is attempting to force or block the kick or play for a return, a definite pattern should be employed. When it is not a sure-kick situation, third-down punt, or field-goal attempt, a sound defense should be used against every offensive possibility except the kick. When the ball is kicked in this situation, a definite punt-return pattern should be used *(Illustration #18)*.

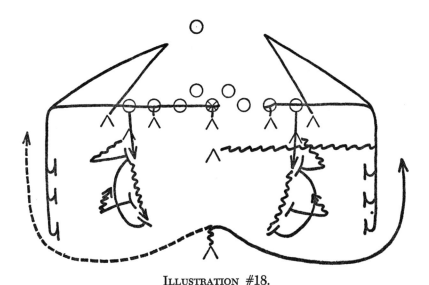

<small>ILLUSTRATION #18.</small>

In attempting to block a kick, every player in the forcing unit must fight to get to the kicker before he can get the ball away. On block kick plays, a pattern is designed to give one man the best opportunity to get through to the kicker. However, you are never sure which man actually will get through to the ball. Since the blocking adjustments of the kicking team may take care of the "theoretically free man", every rusher must go all out to get to the ball. The players rushing the kicker must remember the kicker will move forward as he punts. They must go for a spot approximately three to four yards in front of his original position. If they are rushing from any outside angle, they must cross this spot instead of running directly at the kicker (*Illustration #19*).

Punt returns are based on the execution of these fundamentals by the forcing unit:

1. Certain members of the forcing unit will be assigned to hold up and delay the players opposite them to prevent them from covering the kick quickly.

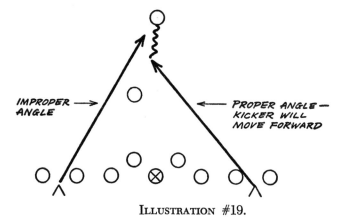

ILLUSTRATION #19.

2. Other players of the unit will be assigned to rush the kicker.
   They can block the kick or tackle the kicker should there be
   a pass from center or a fumble.

3. All men must run an accurate pattern, to a spot twelve yards
   from the sideline and back up the field to set up a wall of
   blockers for the return *(Illustration #20).*

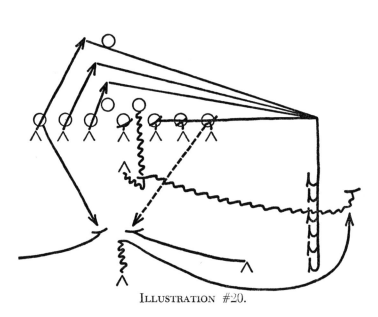

ILLUSTRATION #20.

The most important single factor in a punt return is the players' honest conviction that the play will succeed. The first time the opponent kicks, the forcing unit will make a reasonably good effort to return the punt. However, the kick may be short and no return opportunity develops. This discourages them to the point that on succeeding kicks, they make very little effort to execute the play.

Remember each punt-return play requires the men in the forcing unit to sprint forty yards. They must try hard to return every single punt as they are not sure which kick will be the one that will be returned for a touchdown or a long run, giving their team the ball in scoring position.

CHAPTER FIFTEEN

Defensive Drills

Basic line drills are designed to develop the strength in the hands and arms of linemen as well as body control, agility and the ability to react. The majority of defensive drills for linemen are designed to create a situation which they will face under game conditions.

The following drills are set up in relation to the odd and even defensive alignments and will aid the coaches in selecting players for the different defensive positions.

Block Protection and Reaction Drills

1. ONE VERSUS ONE. The purpose of the one on one drill is to first teach the linemen the four types of block protections. Having learned to execute them, the lineman will know which of the four block protections are best suited for him. He will then concentrate on developing and perfecting them.

In setting up this drill, one half of the men participating in the drill will line up in a straight line approximately two yards apart as offensive men. The other players line up opposite them on defense.

The coach stands behind the defensive players and indicates to the offensive linemen which direction they should block (*Illustration #1*).

The defensive lineman works first from a head-on alignment to control the offensive man. During the drill, the defensive men

COACH

ILLUSTRATION #1.

will work from the various defensive alignments: (1) shade right, control left (2) shade left, control right (3) right shoulder, control left (4) left shoulder, control right.

Change the offensive and defensive men after five or six defensive charges. Change the alignment and charge after all men have worked from the one position. To eliminate having the same men work against each other, rotate the defensive men from left to right after each change of alignment and charge.

The one on one drill will point out to the coach which linemen are able to use their left arm effectively. This will aid him in the placement of personnel, a man who can use his left arm effectively should be able to play on the right side of the defensive line.

2. ONE VERSUS THREE. This drill creates a situation similar to one which the defensive man will actually face under game conditions. It will also indicate to the coach which player may be able to play the middle guard on an odd alignment defense.

The purpose of the drill is to have the defensive lineman learn to react to the movement of the three offensive linemen in his area.

The drill is set up in three groups of four men. Three offensive linemen and one defensive lineman in each group. The coach should place himself behind the defensive players in a position to be able to see all of the men participating in the drill. (*Illustration #2*).

The three offensive men have seven plays: (1) Double team

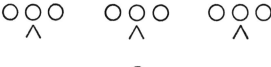

COACH

ILLUSTRATION #2.

block from the left, other linemen pull out in that direction.
(2) Double team block from the right, other linemen pull out in
that direction. (3) The man in front of the defensive man blocks
him to the left, other men pull out in that direction. (4) He may
block him to the right, other men pull out in that direction. (5)
The man in front of the defensive man may block him to the right
or left, other men charge straight ahead. (6) All three men may
block the defensive man to form a wedge. (7) All three men may
drop back executing a pass protection block *(Illustration #3).*

ILLUSTRATION #3.

The coach indicates which of the seven basic movements the
offensive men are to use. He then gives the snap signal and the
players execute them under full-speed game-like conditions.

The men are rotated within their own group so that all four
players have an opportunity to play the defensive position. After
the personnel has been placed in their respective positions, in
this drill only the middle defensive guards will work on defense
against a center and two guards.

3. TWO VERSUS THREE. This drill is set up with the pattern of
an interior even defensive alignment. Again, the placement of
personnel is always kept in mind. The coach is looking for players
who can play the left and right guard positions on an even defensive alignment.

This drill is set up in two groups of five men. Three offensive
linemen and two defensive linemen in each group *(Illustration #4).*

ILLUSTRATION #4.

The three offensive men have nine plays. They are as follows:

1. The No. 1 and 3 men single block the defensive men out and No. 2 man charges straight ahead.

2. The No. 1 and 3 men single block the defensive men to the right or left and No. 2 man charges straight ahead.

3. The No. 2 man blocks the defensive man to his left. The No. 1 man uses an influence block and the No. 3 man traps.

4. The same play to the opposite direction. The No. 2 man blocks the defensive man to his right. No. 3 man influences and No. 1 traps.

5. The No. 2 man blocks the defensive man to his left. The No. 1 man pulls to influence and No. 3 man traps.

6. The same play to the opposite side. The No. 2 man blocks the defensive man to his right. The No. 3 man pulls to influence and No. 1 man traps.

7. The No. 1 and 2 double team block, the No. 3 man single block defensive man out.

8. The No. 2 and 3 double team block, the No. 1 man single block defensive man out.

9. All three men drop back and make pass protection blocks. *(Illustration #5).*

ILLUSTRATION #5.

The coach assumes the same position as in the one versus three and conducts the drill in the same manner.

4. THREE VERSUS FIVE. This drill is set up with the pattern of an interior odd defensive alignment. The purpose of this drill is primarily to teach and to have the defensive linemen learn to react properly to a trap.

Eight linemen participate in the drill. Five offensive linemen and three defensive linemen *(Illustration #6).*

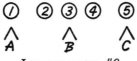

ILLUSTRATION #6.

The five offensive linemen will have five plays to execute. However, the trap play will be run two out of every three plays. These plays are:

1. The No. 2 and 3 men will double team Block B. The No. 1 man will influence A. The No. 4 man will trap A and the No. 5 man single blocks C.

2. Same play in the opposite direction. The No. 3 and 4 men double team B. The No. 5 man influences C. The No. 2 man traps C and No. 1 single blocks A.

3. The No. 1, 3 and 5 men single block to the right, the defensive man in front of them. The No. 2 and 4 men either pull out in that direction or charge straight ahead.

4. The same play in the opposite direction. The No. 1, 3 and 5 men single block to the left, the defensive men in front of them. The No. 2 and 4 men either pull out in that direction or charge straight ahead.

5. All five offensive men drop back and make a pass protection block *(Illustration #7).*

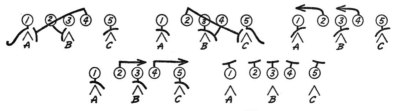

ILLUSTRATION #7.

On a trap play, a double team block is usually used at the point of attack. The opening in the defensive line for the play is actually made by the double team block and not by the trap block.

An advantage of a trap play is that two offensive linemen on the ON side can usually be released, off the line of scrimmage, to block linebackers; and a lineman, the trapper, comes from the offside to block at the point of attack *(Illustration #8)*.

ILLUSTRATION #8.

To play the trap properly, the defensive man to be trapped must close the opening created by the double team block. To do this, he must move laterally off the line of scrimmage toward the double team block, keeping his shoulders parallel to the line of scrimmage. This type of defensive play also makes it more difficult for the trap blocker to execute his block. An offensive gain of two to two and half yards is defensive play against the trap play. *(Illustration #9)*.

ILLUSTRATION #9.

5. FIVE VERSUS SEVEN AND SIX VERSUS SEVEN. These are set up in the same manner as the above drills. The pattern of plays described for the other drills are executed by the offensive men. The defensive men learn to react from the different defensive alignments *(Illustration #10)*.

ILLUSTRATION #10.

6. Seven versus seven. In addition to playing this alignment straight, the different stunts employed from this alignment can be executed during the drill. The stunts are as follows:

1. Cross charge between the two linebackers and the defensive linemen on the tackles *(Illustration #11)*.

ILLUSTRATION #11.

2. Linebacker and linemen on the left side looping to the left to get penetration *(Illustration #12)*.

ILLUSTRATION #12.

3. Linebacker and linemen on the right side looping to the right to get penetration *(Illustration #13)*.

ILLUSTRATION #13.

4. Cross charge between the left linebacker or the right linebacker and the middle man *(Illustration #14)*.

ILLUSTRATION #14.

5. Double cross charge between the two linemen on either side and the linebacker on that side *(Illustration #15)*.

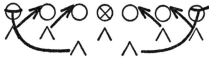

ILLUSTRATION #15.

7. EIGHT VERSUS SEVEN. Four dummies used as backfield men must be used in this drill to have the defensive men learn and execute the stunts from this alignment. The alignment of the dummies will enable the defensive men to take the proper angle on their charges.

The stunts from this alignment are as follows:

1. Cross charge between the linebackers and the defensive linemen on the ends *(Illustration #16)*.

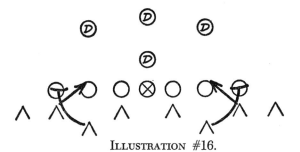

ILLUSTRATION #16.

2. Cross charge between the linebackers and the defensive linemen on the guards *(Illustration #17)*.

ILLUSTRATION #17.

3. Cross charge between the two outside defensive linemen on either side *(Illustration #18)*.

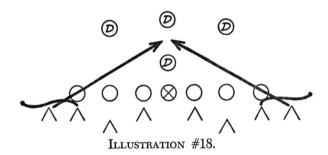

ILLUSTRATION #18.

4. All six defensive linemen charging inside and linebacker covering outside *(Illustration #19)*.

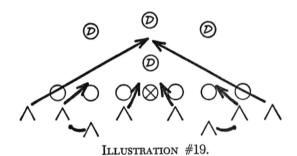

ILLUSTRATION #19.

5. All eight defensive men rushing *(Illustration #20)*.

ILLUSTRATION #20.

After the defensive men have learned the proper foot work and angle of charge to execute the stunts, it is advisable to use a live backfield to run plays. This will enable a defensive man to be able to react out of the stunt charge if, as he stunts, his key tells him he is going away from the play.

After the defensive men have practiced all these drills and have learned to react properly, it is well to use a ball carrier or a full backfield when necessary in the drills. The coach can then be sure that the defensive man is keying properly—the offensive linemen in his area—and not looking into the backfield.

A defensive lineman must discipline himself not to look into the backfield and forget to key the offensive linemen in his area. This will make him vulnerable to the offensive blockers.

Tackling Drills

Tackling is about 75 per cent desire and to have the desire and not know and be able to execute the fundamentals of tackling is almost as bad as to know how and not have the desire to tackle.

We feel the best way to teach and to have the linemen learn to execute the fundamentals of tackling is to do form-half-speed tackling. Our linemen never do any full speed tackling unless it is in a scrimmage or game. Knowing how to tackle is important. If a player knows and can execute the fundamentals and has the desire, he will be able to make the tackle

Since we feel it is necessary to have a variety of drills to accomplish the same thing, we use two tackling drills to have the linemen do their form tackling.

To set up the first tackling drill, the participating players are divided into three groups, ball carriers, ball tossers and tacklers.

Using one of the five yard squares marked in the field, the first ball carrier and tackler line up five yards apart facing in the same direction, the ball carrier behind the tackler. The first ball tosser places himself approximately two yards to the side and 1 yard in front of the tackler. The coach takes his position behind the ball carrier. From this position, he can see whether or not the tackler keeps his eyes open when he is in the area of contact. The tackler must keep his eye open and on the target—the ball—to be able to make a successful tackle *(Illustration #21)*.

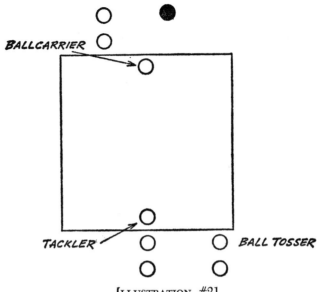

ILLUSTRATION #21.

As the ball tosser tosses the ball to the ball carrier, the tackler turns and moves toward the ball carrier. The ball carrier, after catching the ball, puts it in the proper position and moves towards the tackler. The tackler then makes a half speed form tackle, executing the fundamentals of tackling. The men rotate as follows: ball tosser to tackler, tackler to ball carrier and ball carrier to ball tosser.

The second tackling drill is organized by dividing the participating players into two groups; ball carriers and tacklers. The first ball carrier lines up facing away from the tackler. A football is placed on the ground behind the ball carrier.

The first tackler places himself on the ground on his back five yards from the ball carrier *(Illustration #22).*

On command of hike, given by the coach, the tackler recovers to his feet and moves forward towards the ball carrier. The ball carrier, on the same command, turns around, picks up the ball, puts it in the proper position and moves forward toward the tackler. A form tackle is then made by the tackler.

The fundamentals of tackling as described in Chapter 7 are stressed in both tackling drills. Speed of reaction is also empha-

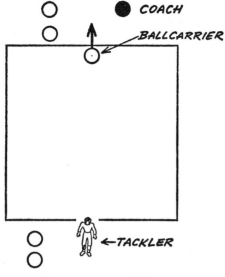

ILLUSTRATION #22.

sized by insisting the tackler makes the tackle mid-way of the five yard distances.

The ball carriers should carry the ball with their left hand and arm half of the time so the tacklers will have to use their left shoulder as well as their right when making the tackle. Each man should make three or four tackles during the drill.

Pursuit Drill

The purpose of the pursuit drill is to have the defensive lineman learn and execute the proper angle of pursuit. One offensive lineman, five defensive linemen and two ball carriers participate in the drill. The first ball carrier lines up five yards behind the center and receives the ball from the center on the snap signal. The four plays for ball carrier to run are: (1) end run right (2) end run left (3) reverse right (4) reverse left. The ball carrier must run ten yards outside the offensive end before turning and running straight up the field.

The coach stands behind the defensive men and indicates which play is to be run. He then calls the snap signal and the play proceeds, with the ball carrier and defensive lineman playing full speed and the offensive lineman executing the proper one on one block half speed. Each defensive man must execute his defensive assignment protecting his territory first. The defensive men in pursuit will then put themselves in a position to tackle the ball carrier by running on the proper angle. Each man must assume a tackling position as he tags the ball carrier.

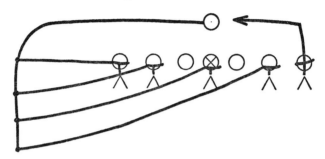

ILLUSTRATION #23—END RUN RIGHT.

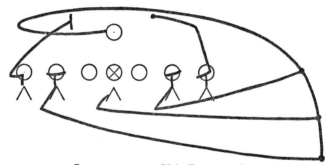

ILLUSTRATION #24—REVERSE LEFT.

Rush Passer Drills (Interception)

The purpose of this drill is to have the defensive linemen learn how to play against the drop back pass and the various plays which may develop from it such as the screen pass, the fake pass and run, and the draw play. The drill also teaches and develops the habit of pursuing the ball when it is thrown. By pursuing the ball, the linemen will put themselves in a position to be blockers should the pass be intercepted, to recover the ball should it be fumbled and to make the tackle from behind should the pass receiver be delayed after he catches the ball.

The drill can be executed with the five defensive linemen in one drill or the players can be divided into two groups, the interior and exterior defensive linemen. By setting the drill up in two groups, the defensive linemen have the opportunity to react more times to the plays for which they are responsible.

The players participating in the exterior group are four left tackles, four right ends, a center and a quarterback. The drill is set up with one end and one tackle on defense. The other three tackles and three ends line up as two offense ends, two screen pass receivers and two defensive halfbacks. The center and quarterback line up normally. *(Illustration #25)*.

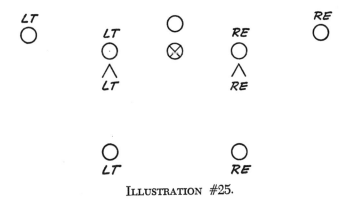

ILLUSTRATION #25.

The plays the quarterback will run are as follows:

1 Throw a screen pass to either side.

2. Fake a pass and run to either side.

3. Throw the pass interception to either defensive halfback.

The coach stands between the defensive halfbacks and indicates to the quarterback which play to execute. The quarterback gives the snap signal and proceeds with the play. The two defensive men react to the play of the quarterback after making their defensive charge.

They react in the following manner:

1. Should the play be to throw the interception to the left defensive halfback, the defensive left tackle comes in and raises his arms so the passer will have to arch the ball making the inter-

ception possible. The right end comes in from the other side
with the intention of tackling the passer. He actually doesn't
tackle the passer in this drill. It is not necessary for him to have
his arms up if the passer is throwing the ball to the other side.

As the passer throws the ball, both players pursue the ball. As
they approach the interceptor, he starts to run with the interception. Both men turn and lead him up the field.

The pass interception to the end is executed in the same manner.
(Illustration #26).

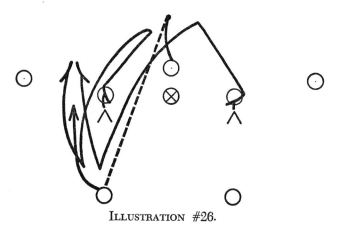

ILLUSTRATION #26.

2. Should the play be the screen pass to the left, the quarterback will drop back ten yards deep as he would on a screen pass
before throwing the ball. The two defensive men will rush the
passer until they recognize that it is a screen pass. This will be
when they are approximately three to four yards deep. They then
react for the screen pass to their side, both men turn and run
to the flat keeping their eyes on the passer. The passer throws
the screen to the left and the pass is either intercepted as the
left tackle as he must be in a position to make the tackle. He
must tag the pass receiver. The screen to the other side is executed
in the same manner *(Illustration #27)*.

3. Should the play be the fake pass and run, the passer fades
back and fakes the pass and attempts to run around the left tackle
or the right end. The four men on each side rotate after four or
five plays until each man has had the opportunity to play as the
defensive man.

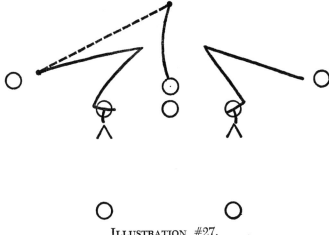

ILLUSTRATION #27.

The right tackles, right guards, left guards, a center and quarterback participate in the interior rush the passer drill.

The interior lineman will play as an offensive fullback, two offensive tackles and two defensive halfbacks. The center and quarterback line up normally. One right tackle and one right guard and one left guard will line up as defense *(Illustration #28)*.

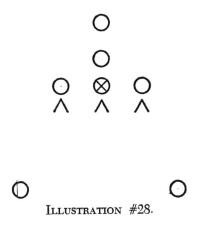

ILLUSTRATION #28.

The purpose of the drill is to have the middle guard learn how to play the draw play and to develop the habit of pursuing the ball after rushing the passer. The three plays the offensive will run are, the draw play and the pass interception to either defensive halfback. The draw play should be run two out of every three plays. The coach stands between the defensive halfback and indicates the play to be run. The quarterback gives the snap count and the play proceeds. The players will react in the following manner:

1. Should the play be the draw, the quarterback drops back and gives the ball to the fullback who attempts to run to either side of the offensive center. The middle guard must stay directly in front of the center, not allowing the center to block him to either side. As the fullback makes his break to either side, the middle guard must move over in front of him in a tackling position and tag him. The other two defensive men who are not responsible for the draw will rush the pass until they are sure he doesn't have the ball. They will then attempt to support on the draw play (*Illustration #29*).

ILLUSTRATION #29.

Should the play be to throw the interception to either defensive halfback, the three must rush the passer, the middle guard does not rush until he is sure it is not the draw play. All three men pursue the ball as the pass is made and become blockers in the same manner that the left tackle and right end do in their drill. (*Illustration #30*).

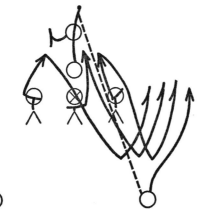

ILLUSTRATION #30.

Split—Shoot the Gap Drill

The purpose of the drill is to have the defensive linemen cut down the splits of the offensive line. Should this not be able to be accomplished, the linemen will shoot the gap any time they feel the split is large enough.

To shoot any gap, the defensive man will line up just inside half the distance and charge for penetration. He will take his first step with his outside foot using an arm lift with his outside arm to protect himself from the outside blocker. An offensive line, five defensive linemen and two linebackers participate in this drill.

The offensive line huddles on each play and after breaking the huddle attempt to split the defensive men. They will close their splits at times and also maintain their splits, allowing the defensive man to shoot the gap. The drill is primarily for the defensive and the offensive line must co-operate *(Illustration #31)*.

ILLUSTRATION #31.

Punt Return Drill

The purpose of this drill is to have the linemen do some running and at the same time execute the punt return. The drill is done at the end of practice when the practice schedule has not included enough running for the linemen.

All the linemen participate in the drill. One line lines up as the offensive line and all the other lines line up, one behind the other, on defense. All centers will be on offensive, one of them being the punter. The punter will go through the act of kicking the ball, but does not punt it so as not to slow up the drill. Two men are placed downfield approximately thirty-five yards.

The coach stands in front of the offensive center and will tell the defensive lines to which side the return will be run. He will then give the snap count and the play will proceed with the defensive linemen executing the punt return.

As the players approach the downfield, he will take a few steps forward so that the linemen will know when to start back upfield. The linemen then sprint another thirty yards up the field and line up behind the last defensive line and await their next turn. The next defensive linemen will run and return to the opposite side. Each line will run five or six returns, which will be 350 to 400 yards of sprinting for each man. At the same time, they are executing something that they will actually do in a game (*Illustration #32*).

The points stressed in the drill are as follows:

1. The three linemen on the side of the return, after executing their defense charge, go straight down the line of scrimmage until they are twelve yards in the side line before turning downfield.
2. After the ball is kicked, the other three linemen who have rushed go to the same spot before going downfield.
3. The men space themselves five yards apart.
4. They must turn to the inside when starting back upfield.

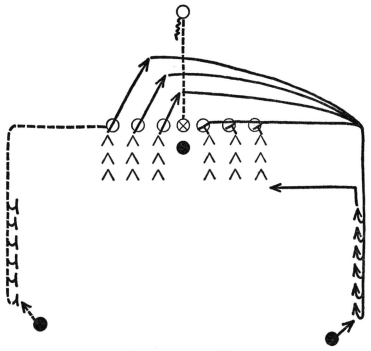

ILLUSTRATION #32.

CHAPTER SIXTEEN

Conclusion

As the game of football has developed and evolved through the years, many theories of offense and defense have become popular only to be replaced by newer concepts. Yet, the fundamentals of the game have remained unchanged.

When I was playing football twenty-five years ago, the single wing and double wing were the dominant offensive formations. A few years later the Shaugnessy T formation became the vogue, offensively. This was followed by the Split T, and more recently, the Winged T and Pro T which utilizes split ends and flankered backs.

Even though the offense in football has undergone all of these various formation changes, the essential maneuvers and individual skills required of linemen have remained unchanged. No matter what the formations of the future may be, the line skills described in this book will remain the basic foundations of successful offensive line play.

Similarly, the defense has undergone constant evolvement. This is a natural development since the defense must adjust to the offensive pattern.

Some 25 years ago almost all football teams used the seven-man line. Occasionally, the center would drop out of the line, and as this trend progressed, the six-man defensive line became the vogue. This was followed by the 5-3 line and the 5-4 or "Oklahoma" defense.

The future will see new alignments and new fundamental theories of team defense. But as was stated concerning offensive football, the fundamentals of defensive line play will remain the same. Thus, the techniques and skills described in this book for defensive line play will remain the foundation on which a successful defense rests.

In conclusion, I would like to make an observation which will explain why I have such tremendous respect for the linemen of football.

These men are literally on the battlefront. Their opponents are well conditioned, strong, aggressive. On each play they are within a yard of each other. Violent contact occurs on every play. If an offensive lineman is successful, some back will run through the hole created by the lineman and get all of the publicity and headlines while the lineman did all of the hard work.

Linemen are literally the unsung heroes of the game. Their situation is analogous to the infantry in warfare. They do the hard, difficult, bitter fighting for victory. As the generals reap the headlines in war, the backs reap the headlines in football. Yet in their hearts, the generals and the backs know that victory and the accolades came to them through the work of the foot soldiers and linemen.

Men that are this willing to sacrifice their own individual identity and their own individual glory to the success of the organization—who unselfishly and unstintingly give their entire mental and physical resources so that their organization may succeed are made of the stuff from which true greatness derives.

In all human endeavors, the "linemen's attitude" is necessary. When the linemen succeed in winning their battle, the organization succeeds.

Thus, the great education in football is in this spirit of team play and self-sacrifice which is so well personified by the devotion to the team shown by every lineman.